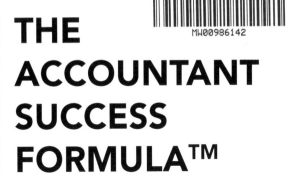

THE ACCOUNTANT SUCCESS FORMULA™

FREEING TODAY'S ACCOUNTANT FROM AN OPPRESSIVE BUSINESS MODEL

ERIK SOLBAKKEN, CPA

Norsemen Books

THE ACCOUNTANT SUCCESS FORMULA™

Also issued in electronic format

ISBN 9781657258273

Published by Norsemen Books www.NorsemenBooks.com

Contents

Dedication

In part, I dedicate this book to the accounting profession itself. Sometimes, those that hurt us most, teach us best. Thank you for teaching me to question the status quo. When we do, we can find a whole new world of amazing possibilities.

To my wife Erin, thank you for always supporting and believing in me. From changing our accounting practice to changing the accounting profession, you've always been there to help make it happen.

And finally, to all the accountants out there who are sick and tired of being overworked and undervalued. Your time has come. You don't have to live this way anymore. This book is for you.

Prologue

I have good news and bad news.

The bad news is that you're practicing a model of business that is oppressive, suffocating, and of your own doing.

The good news is that I've been in that hole before, and I know the way out.

As you read the content in the pages that follow, they are going to seem, at times, uncomfortably familiar. I too spent a large portion of my career as an accountant buying into the fact that part of my profession meant chasing billable hours, working into the night, and struggling with clients to pay me for work I had already completed.

Only when I finally considered leaving the industry was I able to develop, implement, and become successful in what has now become the new model for accountants.

The Accountant Success Formula™ principles outline the tested and proven techniques to transition a traditional accounting practice into one that represents the needs of today's accountant and the ideal clients they wish to serve.

Join me as we set the traditional business model on fire.

Yours in success,

Erik

CHAPTER 1: A Proud and Noble Profession

In the Beginning...

It was 1987. My hair was long, with a perm and highlighted. Technically, I had a mullet. But it was a cool mullet (if that's a possible statement) due to the extras I had added to it. Of course, I had to play the part, because I was the drummer and lead singer in a heavy metal band. I loved that 80s hair metal music. Still do.

I was sitting by my locker in the common area of my high school, trying to decide what courses to take for my last semester of Grade 12. I did well academically, so clearly it was expected that I would go to university after graduation. Only one problem...I had no idea what I wanted to do.

Remember that pressure? To answer that all-encompassing question as an adolescent: "What do you want to be when you grow up?" Honestly, I think I'm still trying to figure out the answer. Does anyone ever really know? But that's a question to be covered in an entirely different book.

As I was thumbing through the pages of the available courses, I came across the descriptions for Accounting 11 and Accounting 12. Both were half courses, so I could easily fit them into my last semester. I was (and still am) a bit of an anomaly. I loved math (a numbers geek) and I loved playing heavy metal rock music (a cool kid). So I thought hey, worth a shot to see what this accounting thing is all about.

After a few weeks and the first "aced test" I realized that I could use my inherent math skills to have a career. I could finally answer that damn question about what I wanted to be when I grew up! It was nirvana for a numbers geek. My inner cool kid was okay with this because of rationalization. I could first become an accountant (to have a solid, steady career and income) and then start my heavy metal rock star career (because I'd have the cash to support it).

The funny thing is, this actually happened. Not the way I expected it to, but it did happen. I was hell bent on becoming an accountant…and I did. I was hell bent on becoming partner in the accounting firm I articled at…and I did. Then I was hell bent on firing up that heavy metal rock band career…and I did (but again, that's definitely a story for a different book).

Why this trip down memory lane? Is it because I want to tell you about my wicked hairstyle back in the day or brag about being in a heavy metal rock band? No. This is a book about how to update the business model you're using in your accounting practice.

Somewhere, back in your history, was the moment you decided to become an accountant. If you're like me, it was a very important day, probably filled with excitement and anticipation. Can you remember where you were and how you felt the day you decided to join this proud and noble profession? More importantly, do you still have the same feeling of nirvana today as you did when you started on this journey? Is your inner numbers geek still happy and excited to go to work? Are you still really happy with your decision to become an accountant?

For the practitioners I meet, the answer is a resounding no. It becomes an even more explicative no if you ask these questions around tax time. And people say accountants don't have strong personalities. They'll come out of their shells if you push the right buttons at the wrong time of year. I remember one tax season, throwing clients out of my office while shouting some rather profane language at them. Oh and just to be clear, I didn't physically throw them out of my office (even though I visualized it).

What happened between that day you decided to become an accountant and today? Why are so many accountants bitter and frustrated with their careers? The answer is simple...the profession happened. A profession that believes in the old-school business model of grinding out billable hours and working crazy overtime is the norm. As much as we love to call ourselves "forward-thinking problem solvers" for our clients, when it comes to our own businesses, we've failed miserably. We do, however, share this fault equally with the profession. We've accepted the old-school business model as the way things are supposed to be. We've accepted the status quo, and that there is change. We've accepted this career-long cross as something we must just bear. It's all bullshit.

It's a basic function of human nature to not like change. Look around you and you can see groups of people fighting to the death to maintain their way of thinking. It's happened throughout history, and no group is more stuck in their ways than the accounting profession. They too will fight to the death defending their status quo.

In this book, I'm going to share with you the how this inability to evolve has not only affected your quality of life in the past, but how it's holding you back today and what it's going to do to you in the future. In Charles Darwin's theory of evolution, species that evolve to their changing environments continue their lineage, and those who don't...die off. The same fate will happen to accountants if we don't change. Those who stay in the status quo and feverishly defend their way of thinking will become extinct. While those who embrace change, evolve, and accept a new, updated business model will survive and thrive in their new world.

The Past, Present and Future

Let's take a brief look at the history of the accounting profession and where it is today and try to make some reasonable predictions as to what the future will bring. If Darwin's theory holds true, we'll not only want to look where we're heading, but what course corrections are required if we want to survive.

The Past

As accountants, we've been highly trained in the art of analyzing the past. Almost everything we do is based on review of past transactions, compiling historical accounts to create financial statements and prepare tax filings. As such, it seems very fitting that we take the same skillset and actually apply it to our own profession to find out what the hell went wrong. We're highly educated and skilled professionals, right? Let's put it to good use.

When you look back in time and study the history of accounting, you'll see that not much has changed. From the pictures of Bob Cratchit working like a dog for Ebenezer Scrooge (hunched over his file work) to today's accountant working like a dog (hunched over their file work), the landscape really doesn't look that different. Bob Cratchit had a billable hour quota to reach, and so does today's modern accountant. Other than the quality of the actual workspace, nothing much has really changed. Where most industries have been required to evolve and adapt to survive, somehow the accounting profession has managed to remain stagnant with its old-school business model.

I'm sure some of you are going to say that that's not true. "What about computers? Where Bob Cratchit had to handwrite journal entries and manually complete tax filings for Ebenezer's clients, today's accountant has the luxury of the power of technology. Computers have made a huge jump in the evolution of the profession. Where Bob was considered a slave to the grind, today's accountant is free as a bird!"

This may seem a true statement; however, when you look closer, you'll see this hasn't been the case. I remember my first articling position, where we had only three computers in the entire office of over 18 people (there was one for the reception and two for the rest of the accounting staff). I remember the insane overtime we used to do during tax season. Back then, we never actually used those computers for preparing tax returns. We just used them for bookkeeping and some internal financial statement preparation. The personal tax returns were first compiled by handwritten computer sheets, and then we'd walk those sheets over to a third-party data-processing center. The next day, we'd walk back and pick up the printed tax returns and check them for accuracy. If they were wrong, we'd have to manually write changes on the computer sheets, walk them back to the data-processing center, and wait until the next day to get the re-printed return.

Fast-forward to today and you'll see a computer and printer/scanner on every single desk in the office. Information slips are scanned or automatically uploaded to the tax preparation software and checked for accuracy within minutes, not days. Technology saves the day, right? Look closer. If we've been able to reduce the workload so much, then why are accountants still logging crazy overtime during tax season? Shouldn't we be able to put our feet up and relax now that technology is doing the work for us? Why are we still working like this?

It's partially due to conditioning. Accountants have always worked like this, so we think we should continue to work like this...forever. Like Pavlov's dog, every time the bell rings for food, the dog starts salivating. With the accountant, the workday starts, ring the bell, work like a dog! Maintain the status quo to the death, and to hell with evolution!

The other big reason we continue to work this way is the effect increases in efficiency have on the price of a product or service. I'll go into this in much more detail later on when I talk about the Value Curve, but for now let's just look at how technological advances affect price. Industry-specific advances make things easier and less costly to produce and, in an open market, this translates into lower prices for the consumer. Take a quick scan online and you'll see that items you couldn't afford in the past are now being sold for pennies on the dollar.

Think about personal tax returns. Where have prices gone over the last 30 years? Have prices followed inflation? Not even close. Clearly, labour costs and overhead have increased dramatically, so why hasn't the price of tax returns done the same? It's due to the technology. Returns are way quicker and easier to produce than ever before. These increases in efficiency have put downward pressure on the price.

The Present

Technology is changing so rapidly that today's newest and greatest innovation will literally be tomorrow's dinosaur. Many of the technologies I'll mention in this book may not even exist in a few years' time. Many more new technologies will have already come and gone as well. What is essential is that we look to see what technology is doing (and is going to do) to our profession and how we can prepare ourselves for these changes.

Outsourcing

Many would say that outsourcing is "technically" not a technology. It is, however, an issue you need to be aware of. Technology has played a significant part in how outsourcing has impacted many markets and professions. From personal assistants to even medical advice, the world market has opened up, and lower-cost labour is undermining local services.

I can easily post almost any service-based job on multiple crowd-sourced websites and have literally hundreds of highly skilled people in third-world countries bidding on it. For pennies on the dollar, I can have my website built, appointments managed, or even a medical diagnosis made. The same thing is happening in the accounting profession.

I regularly receive emails from accountants in India and Pakistan offering their services to local accounting firms. Again, you'd think this would be great for us—more offloading of work. We can outsource even more of what we were doing in the past and put our feet up. It should be like the coming of summer. The days are continually getting brighter and warmer. Blue skies ahead, right?

If you've taken any economics courses, it doesn't take long to figure out what this will do to your market segment. With this inflow of outsourcing and lower-priced options, the accounting profession will feel even more downward pressure on pricing. Eventually the market catches up and will seek out those firms undercutting prices due to the reduced costs inside their model. This means that even if you don't outsource, you're still going to have to compete with lower-priced competition. Hello, more downward pressure on price. Isn't outsourcing great!

Outside Competition

With the introduction of new technologies comes another risk to the accounting industry. Companies and other professions are now seeing an opportunity to take away market share from us. With the ability to process tax returns with automated software, many people who were never qualified to do so are now able to play in our proud and noble sandbox.

During my time in public practice, I was fortunate enough to buy my own office space and move into a strata complex where multiple businesses operated. The first week we moved in, I went around and introduced myself to the other tenants. A good-neighbour policy is always the best policy. I was expecting a warm reception and a loving embrace, for they would know that I wasn't a rowdy neighbour, right? I was from a proud and noble profession! What I wasn't prepared for was how many of these non-accounting businesses were actually doing some form of accounting work.

Both financial advisors firms and, believe it or not, even a law firm told me they were taking care of some of their clients' bookkeeping and tax filings. I was in a state of shock. How dare they play in my sandbox! They actually told me their business plan was to put a fence around the client. To take care of all those services they needed. Talk about not playing nice. I don't mean to sound like a broken record, but remember what happens when you get more competition in an industry? Yes, that's right, downward pressure on price.

Automation

The accounting profession is ripe for poaching by technological solutions. Manual services are being replaced at an alarming rate by advances in technology. Many accountants have argued in the past (and continue to argue) that no computer can replace them. Sounds like the same thing the automobile factory worker said decades ago. Where are they now? Investment advisors also said robo-investors weren't a threat either…until they were.

Many of the big firms have been reducing their staffing requirements and replacing them with automated auditing software. No more need to manually test samples and prepare statistical analysis by real people. We've got technology for that. It's not only cheaper, but it's also more reliable and accurate. Talk about reducing your audit risk.

Bookkeeping online software-as-a-service is big business as well. Platforms such as Xero, QuickBooks Online, and Sage have taken off like wildfire. The number of third-party plug-ins to make the job even easier is mind-blowing. What used to take hours of manual entry is now done automatically, in real time. Soon our job is going to be done for us, and we can sit back and relax, right? Hmmm…I think I need to get out my sunscreen, it's getting a little too warm. I might get sunburnt.

Subscription-Based Model

Outside of the technology changes, there's another trend worth mentioning. The movement away from the one-time payment to the subscription-based model. Netflix, Apple Music, and Xero are just a few examples. Almost all software-as-a-service offerings have gone to this model. People love it. It smoothens cash flow and hurts much less when they open their wallet. The purchasing decision becomes easier, and they enjoy the services even more because of it.

Businesses love this model as well. Cash is king, and having a consistent monthly cash flow is critical to any business. The monthly subscription model is about as smooth as it gets. Once a customer is locked in, businesses can do cash-flow projections with much more certainty and accuracy. Also, the number of eyeballs using their services increases their business value. More opportunities for cross offers, advertising revenues, and strategic partnerships become available when you have millions of users. The subscription-based model becomes a win-win scenario, and it's picking up steam. As I'll demonstrate later on, this model is not only powerful for businesses with millions of users; it's also incredibly lucrative when implemented correctly inside an accounting practice.

The Future

Given our past history with the profession, and seeing the changes in the current landscape, what can we predict about our future? Any business owner, in any market segment, who doesn't look to future changes and try to anticipate where things are headed, is doomed to fail. They're like an ostrich with their head stuck in the sand saying nothing's wrong when there's a storm headed their way.

We can easily look to the past to see where entire industries have been wiped out—almost to the point of extinction—because of this lack of vision of where everything was heading. Trends on how customers want to consume products or services can't be ignored. Given my love of heavy metal music, I can't help but think of the music industry as a prime example. The big music companies thought they had the market tied up and were incredibly protective of their position. Instead of embracing the trend of people wanting to openly share their music, they tried to control the situation.

When you used to go to concerts, they would do a body search and take away any recording devices you had on you. You were strictly prohibited from taking any picture or video of any live performances. I remember where Axl Rose of Guns n' Roses actually walked off the stage at one of his concerts because he was so pissed off that someone was simply taking a picture of him. A major riot broke out in the crowd as a result.

Isn't that insane given today's free sharing of video and pictures online? Instead of seeing a bunch of cigarette lighters in the air during a slow song, you now see smart phone screens. Everybody is recording and posting everything! It's what people wanted, and that's what they got. They wanted to openly share their experiences and the things they liked with whomever, wherever they were.

These major recording labels no longer have a chokehold on the industry. Artists are easily able to record and distribute their music via open-sourced online forums and platforms. Music is now openly shared between friends. Also, instead of having the cost of buying an entire album, you can easily purchase a monthly subscription service for even less and have access to thousands of records.

Change happens. What used to be the norm is now considered ridiculous. What used to be a lucrative and protected market segment is now an open-source free-for-all. The combination of technological advances and customer consumption preferences are the contributing factors. Let's learn from the past and present and see where we can start to predict what changes are going to happen to our proud and noble profession.

Technology

Clearly, we can see that most, if not all, of our current software upgrades are designed to improve the efficiencies upon which accountants can perform their tasks. The focus is on how to get things done quicker to reduce human labour costs. Get it done quicker and we can improve our margins, right?

In addition to getting things done quicker, technology is removing the human error component to file preparation. Remove the human, and you remove the human error. Technology doesn't have a bad day, or have a spat with their spouse, or get pissed off at their superior. A sunny afternoon outside doesn't distract a computer software program from accurately preparing the necessary calculations to get the job done.

We're already seeing staffing requirements in the large accounting firms dropping due to audit software. What used to take hundreds of labour hours can now be automated through imbedded audit software. No more manual samples needed during the interim and year-end audit procedures anymore.

Simply have the software collect and analyze it all for us in a matter of minutes. This is clearly not a trend that's going away. It's going to accelerate.

Artificial Intelligence

On the old TV show Star Trek, one of the reasons for the Enterprise's mission was to seek out new life and civilizations, to boldly go where no one has gone before. Clearly we are doing this in real life as well. Instead of travelling the universe at light speed and setting our phasers to stun, however, we are looking at creating life itself here on earth through AI (artificial intelligence). Yes…I'm a closet science-fiction geek as well, except I much prefer Star Wars to Star Trek (again, another "polarizing" subject for a future book).

The ability to have computer software increase the efficiency of our tasks and remove the human error is only the tip of the iceberg. What computer programmers and scientists all over the world are trying to do is to get our computers to think and problem solve just like us humans—except better. The question is if technology not only increases efficiency, accuracy, and problem solving, then where does that leave us human accountants?

Before you start laughing and saying there's no way AI can replace you, look at this list of people who were also told that their ideas were insane. They were told that their vision of reality, of the future, was flawed. What was previously considered ridiculous is now an undisputed fact:

The world is round – Galileo

We can fly – The Wright Brothers

We can have light without a flame – Thomas Edison

Machines will never replace a human – The factory assembly line worker

AI is coming, and it's going to change our view of the world yet again. It has the power to eliminate entire market segments, and many people will find themselves out of a job. Even accountants.

Block Chain

As I was writing this book, one of the newest technologies to arise was Block Chain. Block Chain has taken automated bookkeeping software advances and made them look like a cute beginner's game. Where the ease and convenience of automated bookkeeping software functions has reduced the need for human labour, Block Chain has opened up the potential for completely eliminating the need for it altogether.

In simple terms, Block Chain technology is a digital ledger in which economic transactions are recorded both chronologically and publicly. It was originally created for managing digital currency transactions, but its application is finding its way into many other areas. Unlike traditional accounting software that only records one party's side of the transaction (for example, the purchaser), Block Chain records both sides (purchaser and buyer).

Picture a world in which all transactions are not only permanently recorded, but are automatically verified by all parties in the transaction. Putting effort into ensuring your clients' books and records were correct will be replaced with a "real-time" verifiable and incorruptible ledger. They'll be no question whether your client actually bought that piece of machinery. If it's in the Block Chain, it happened.

What does this mean for the future of the profession? It doesn't take much of a stretch to envision a world ledger where all transactions are automatically populated without our help. Governments could have access and be able to audit (in real time) all economic transactions in their constituents' businesses. Gone are the days of needing a third-party intermediary (like an accountant) to pull together the financial information necessary to file tax returns.

Okay, so now I'm certain I've lost some of you. I'm sure you're saying, "This all sounds really interesting, Erik, but you're painting a future where Big Brother is watching everything that we do. You're going off the deep end into science fiction." Maybe I am, or maybe I'm not. The point of this discussion isn't to get into a debate over the future but rather get us thinking about where everything is headed. To survive in this business, you need to not only keep your eye on today's activities, but you need to keep your eye on the ball of what's likely coming. Preparation and adoption is key to survival. Resistance is futile.

Thinking about the Future

Let's recap what we've covered so far to spur us to think about our future and where we're heading, and to ensure everyone is on the bus as we move forward.

#1 – Technological advances are reducing the need for human labour. Increased efficiencies and accuracy are the gains. The losses are the reduced reliance on "warm bodies" to do the job. More technology. Fewer humans.

#2 – Consumers are embracing and expecting subscription-based models. Consumers love knowing exactly how much something is going to cost ahead of time and being able to pay for it in smaller monthly increments. In addition, the convenience of the set-and-forget payment system reduces the consumer's need to continually make buying decisions. Businesses that have embraced this model are reaping the rewards as well. Win-win all around. Everyone is happy.

It doesn't take much thought to see what the future holds for accounting firms. Technology and customer consumption preferences are shining a big spotlight on the road ahead. Before we start taking this road to the solution, however, we have to deal with the elephant in the room first. The first step to recovery is recognizing there's a problem. In the case of the accounting profession, there's more than just one.

There are two major problems with the traditional business model that need to be addressed. Interestingly enough, the traditional model is so ingrained in the profession, so conditioned, that most accountants resist even talking about it, let alone doing something to fix it. Completely unwilling to evolve and adapt, many will fight to the death to protect the status quo. Those who do change, who do evolve, are not only going to survive, they are going to thrive.

Two Major Problems

Changes in technology and customer consumption preferences have not only shone a light on the future, they've shone a light on the two biggest problems with the traditional business model used by accounting firms. These two offenders are not only problems; they are the exact root of all evil with the profession itself. Stamp these out and you'll find yourself in a whole new world of possibilities and freedom you never dreamed of.

Who are these two horsemen of the apocalypse? They are:

1) Reliance on Compliance Filings, and
2) The Billable Hour

Compliance Filings

Most accounting practices are heavily reliant on compliance filings. This only makes sense. It's been our bread and butter for centuries. The need to report and file our clients' economic activities with the relevant government authorities is the bedrock of the accounting profession. You may say it's the reason the profession exists in the first place. So, how are we going to deal with the one very thing that puts food on the table for us? We'll see the solution soon enough, but for now, let's take a look at the Value Curve to help provide even more insight into exactly what's going on here.

The Value Curve

What is a Value Curve?

A Value Curve is a diagram, which can be used to show instantly where value is created within an organization›s products and services. It shows graphically the way a company or an industry configures its consumer offering. I first came across the Value Curve, as it relates to the accounting profession, during my research to find a new way to run my own practice. More specifically, I found it while reading an insights paper created by Ric Payne, the co-founder of Results Accountants' Systems and he has very graciously given me permission to use his illustration to share with you throughout the book (thank you Ric!). The Value Curve highlighted an essential key to what was happening to me and so many other accountants, worldwide. This key to a successful accounting firm business model may seem like common sense once we discuss it. The real trick however, is applying this common sense to produce uncommon results.

The Value Curve illustrates the interaction between the types of services you provide relative to your client's price sensitivities. It also shows how increases in drive prices downward, whereas increases in efficiency drive prices downward, whereas increases in effectiveness upward.

Key Items:

Value Curve = Services Provided
Horizontal Axis = Compliance (Commodity Service) vs. Reliance (Value Added Service)
Vertical Axis = Client's Price Sensitivity
Efficiency vs. Effectiveness as it relates to Price

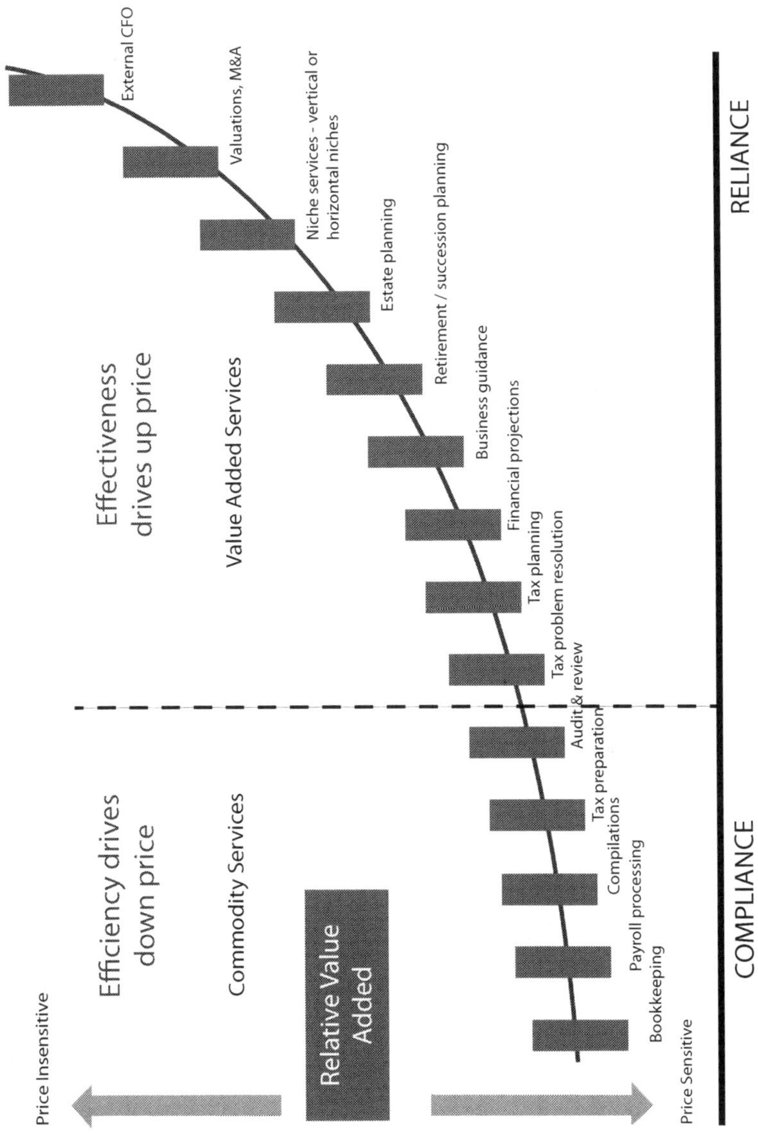
Price Insensitive
Efficiency drives down price
Commodity Services
Relative Value Added
Price Sensitive
Bookkeeping
Payroll processing
Compilations
Tax preparation
Audit & review
Tax problem resolution
Tax planning
Financial projections
Business guidance
Retirement / succession planning
Estate planning
Niche services - vertical or horizontal niches
Valuations, M&A
External CFO
Effectiveness drives up price
Value Added Services
COMPLIANCE
RELIANCE

The services provided on the left-hand side of the curve are the most price sensitive in the eyes of our clients, whereas the services provided to the right are less price sensitive. Whenever we get to work on projects that are further to the right of the curve, we are able to charge much more with less resistance from our clients. It's common sense, right?

What's also true, from an economic modeling standpoint, is that when any product or service becomes easier (less expensive) to produce, the price drops. Technology advances have helped speed up that downward trend, haven't they? Again, even more common sense.

What doesn't make sense is why most accounting firms are consumed with how to increase efficiencies in their firms. Why aren't they looking to be more *effective*? That's where the best value is for our clients, and it commands the highest price we can receive for our services.

Let's picture this one-two punch. Traditionally, firms have been heavily reliant on compliance filings, which are the most price-sensitive services we can provide. Combine this with a focus on increasing efficiencies, which accelerates the downward pressure on prices. Technology is getting to the point where it's starting to do much of this stuff for us. What's going to happen to prices then? It's like we're pushing a snowball down a hill toward our homes, and it's getting bigger and faster with every push. Can anyone say avalanche?

The Billable Hour

Of the two horsemen, the billable hour is the nastiest. To get accountants to see the compliance-filing trap and to embrace the Value Curve dynamics is easy compared to moving this bad boy. Volumes of books have been written just on this subject alone. The first book I read on the subject, and which I consider as the Holy Grail, was written by Paul Dunn and Ron Baker, called *The Firm of The Future*. I wouldn't be doing it justice to dedicate only a few paragraphs to discuss the billable hour.

We've been so conditioned to accept the billable hour, this status quo, as gospel that many of us can't see straight. Common sense falls away and we're left with fierce debate. Many accountants act as if we're committing a sin to even talk about leaving this part of the traditional business model behind.

The real sin is not looking to where the market is headed and ignoring it.

The real sin is pretending nothing's wrong.

The real sin is not evolving.

The real sin is protecting the status quo because it's the status quo.

The real sin is defending our position…to the death.

Since I've taken us down this path of the sinner, let's look at how these two evils combine forces to commit the real sins on our proud and noble profession.

CHAPTER 2: Sins of the Traditional Model

Bad Relationships

Markets grow, change, and evolve. In most cases, the key to all growth is pain. Pain is the major motivator for change. What is equally true is how much tolerance for pain humans have. They'll stay in one place without changing regardless of the levels of pain and suffering they're experiencing, just to keep the comfort of the regular and the known. They harden and become callous.

Ever witness a friend going through a nasty relationship? They whine and complain about how painful it is being with the person, yet they won't end the relationship. They stay in pain because the thought of the unknown, a different person to have a relationship with or loneliness, is more painful than staying in the one they already are in. They stay suffering because of a fear of change. What inevitably happens is that the pain of staying in the relationship becomes too much to bear, and they eventually leave. They are "forced out".

The traditional business model used in accounting firms is that bad relationship. It treats us like shit, but we stay anyway because we normalize to it. Eventually however, the pain of this relationship will be too much, and people will wake up and leave. Sometimes the catalyst is simply talking to a friend and having them point out exactly what's going on. They point out the sins that are being committed against us, and then the pain becomes obvious and heightened. Sadly, many leave the profession or go in-house rather than adapting their practice. They didn't have a friend to remind them there was another option.

I'm that friend for you right now. I'm going to point a spotlight on these professional crimes committed against you. Remember not to shoot the messenger. This relationship is yours, not mine. I'm simply a friend who understands, because I too was once stuck in that hole, but…I found the way out. The current relationship between you and your practice is toxic. It is co-dependent. It's treating you terribly, and you are accepting it. Between compliance filings and billable hours, you can't help but get ground down. When we know better, we do better, and accepting "what is" is the first step of moving toward "what can be". First, let's identify all the sins.

Sin #1 – Charging on Time vs. Value

I'm going to begin by hitting the nail right on the head. Out of the two horsemen, the billable hour is the worst. It chains us to the desk, treats us like a slave to the grind, and holds us back so we can't rise to our true potential. It holds us back and tells us we can't hang out and have fun with our friends. It tells us we have to stay at home and do the chores around the house. No fun for you, it says (yikes...I'm already having flashbacks).

Nothing keeps accountants' earnings capped like the billable hour. There are only so many hours in the day, and once you've chosen your charge-out rate, you're capped at how much you can earn. The only way to increase your earnings is to work more hours. Bill more time! Bill more time! Bill more time!

This is the point where many accountants, stuck in the fog of this relationship, pull out their calculators and say, "Let's just raise our billable rates!" Great idea…you think. But what do your clients think of this great idea when you tell them this? "You charge how much per hour?!" they scream. Every time we raised our rates in my first firm, it was really difficult to have that conversation, especially with existing clients. Kind of like vomit getting stuck in your throat. I thought I heard one of my partners gagging once when they were having a client discussion about this.

This is also where the combination of forces creates the nightmare for us. With a capped income, we're forced to work longer hours to make what we want to make. Couple that with the downward price pressure on compliance filings, and the volume requirement increases yet again. Perfect storm. Accountants are working just as long and tedious hours as they ever have in the past, only now they're expected to produce much more work than ever before due to increases in efficiencies.

What's the other solution? "Let's hire more accountants so we can bill out more chargeable hours!" I can hear someone shout. Good work, someone did the math. Welcome to the complexity of human dynamics and scaling your practice. More staff = more complexity = more headaches. I've seen smaller practitioners make three times more money than partners in bigger firms when they've moved to a value-pricing model. Not only that, they experience way less administrative headaches, and they have a smile on their face, even during tax season.

Another "wonderful" by-product (sarcasm intended) of charging for time vs. value is that it lures accountants into focusing on filling their day with hours. Time and time again, in practices all over the world, accountants have a client inventory full of low-value work. "It doesn't matter", they shout, "it's all billable time and I can get paid for it!" Reminds me of another profession that accepts money for service. It's the "oldest" profession in the history of human kind. I'll let you do that to me…for a price. Again, this leads to the volume issue arising. If you take on low-value work, you need higher volume to make your revenue targets. Go back to the Value Curve, and we see the snowball effect. Price sensitivity, increases in technology, further price sensitivity, need for higher volumes, accepting even more low-value work. So much fun, right?

The last point I'll make on this sin is the benefits some of your clients receive as a result of your services. Focusing on the chargeable hour has no relevance to the actual value they receive. Where one client could come in and get an hour of advice from you and use that to save $100 in taxes, another person may save $100,000. Way to capture the value you've created for your clients! Professionals who work on a commission basis snicker at accountants about this aspect of our chargeable hour model. I remember working hard through a business transaction and the related income tax returns, only to see what the other professionals involved were making on the deal. "They got paid what? What the hell am I doing here at 10:00 at night slaving away for a fraction of the spoils? Life's not fair."

Sin #2 – Selling Stuff vs. Transformation

With our training and obsession on our billable hour comes the second of our sins—selling based on the stuff we do vs.

the transformation our clients receive. One of the first things we learned as accounting students was how to fill out our time sheet. The billable hour is the driver of our business, is what we were told. "If you don't account for every hour, the world will end!" As such, we've been conditioned to think of the billable hour as the alpha and the omega.

We focus on the inputs as the most important aspect of our business model. I can hear the chant, "It's all about the time, it's all about the time, it's all about the time!" Almost cult-like, really. Yikes…I just had another flashback, with chills going down my spine. Like programmed robots, our training has us conditioned to do the march, grind out the hours, and do the time. "Time, time, time!"

This obsession has another major negative side effect. It's one that's very subtle, one that most accountants never realize. They can go their entire career without having the slightest idea that they're missing the most critical skill to all business success. That skill is the ability to sell. Most accountants don't have a clue how to sell effectively. It's not their fault really, they've never been taught this skill. They've been too busy filling out their time sheet.

Remember the tax return on the sales transaction? Now those people know how to sell. Commissioned sales people have to know how to sell, that's their job. If they don't sell, they don't eat, plain and simple. Accountants on the other hand…eh, not so much.

Flash in your mind to an accountant sitting down with a new client prospect and having the sales conversation. The accountant is showing off their tax skills and knowledge to show the client how amazing they are. They talk about all the things they are going to do for the client. They go into ridiculous detail about the complexities of their prospect's situation. "Aha, I've got them scared now", thinks the accountant. "They really need me. This sales conversation is going great. The client is scared out of his pants. They're definitely going to sign on."

Inevitably the client asks the question, "How much will this cost?" The accountant then squirms and says, "Well it all depends on the time and complexity involved, blah blah blah." Oh shit, thinks the client, this is going to be expensive. Right there, BOOM, you've set up the relationship for life. If they do end up signing on, they will always see you as a cost. Accountant leads to cost…cost leads to pain…pain leads to suffering (and for those Star Wars fans out there, yes, that was my Yoda plug).

The client is always going to think, from this day forward, I hope it doesn't take them long to do this job, I want to keep my suffering to a minimum. For them, going to the accountant is like going to the dentist to have their wisdom teeth pulled. Necessary, but seriously sucks. I know this is going to hurt, but I have to do this, they think. The accountant becomes the necessary evil in their life.

This brilliant sales approach also upsets the laws of the Value Curve universe when you're having a sales conversation about a value-added service. What should have been price insensitive has now been shifted down the left side of the Value Curve and has become a price-sensitive service in the eyes of your prospective client. Like the dark side of the force, twisting and shaping good to evil, so we see these lucrative opportunities reduced to price-sensitive, commodity-like services.

Well done. Good sales job!

Yes…that definitely was sarcasm.

You've now positioned yourself in a conflict of interest with your client. Yes, you heard me correctly, a conflict of interest. Talk about having a shiver running up and down your spine. Our proud and noble profession is in a conflict of interest? "Never!" you scream, but let's think about it. Throughout this fantastic sales conversation, the client's interest is to have the accountant spend the least amount of time on their file, whereas the accountant's interest (being a business owner) is to maximize their revenues. Having a billable hour model means the only way to maximize revenues is to maximize chargeable time. Yet your client wants you to minimize your time.

Conflict of interest.

By selling the "stuff" that we do and not the transformation (the value received), we create a world of problems. These problems continue throughout the life cycle of the client relationship. It's the gift that just keeps on giving, but it's the type of gift you really don't want. Like getting a sweater from Grandma on your birthday when you were a kid. The worst part is, it's a gift accountants give themselves. Ironic, isn't it?

Sin #3 – Billing after the Fact

This sin should have its own book, never mind a section of a chapter. However, the goal with this book wasn't to give you yet another huge volume of work to digest. You get enough of that with all the tax law changes and updates to reporting standards you have to do each and every year. No, the purpose of this chapter is to simply put the spotlight on those dark corners of our profession that no one wants to look at. Like actors in a horror movie who can't see the monsters hiding in the corners, when the entire audience can clearly see the dangers, accountants simply march on through without a clue. The only reason accountants can't see them is because they've become so ingrained in us through hundreds of years of conditioning that the consequences of living with monsters just feels normal.

Billing after the fact is no exception. Grinding through a client's file, determining the billable hours after the fact, agonizing over what to charge, writing off WIP, presenting a bill, and then chasing the client for the outstanding receivable is normal, right? It totally makes sense that we chase the money after we've done the work, that's why we went to school for so long.

Billing after the fact not only causes more stress than is really necessary, it takes all control out of our hands and puts it squarely into the hands of our clients. Where we should be having a mutually beneficial economic transaction, we've tipped the scales of the power to the client. We spend the time, do all the work, agonize over what to charge, and then basically hope our clients accept the charges. "Please, please, please don't question the bill", is what runs through our head as we present the invoice. It removes our power and puts the client in control. We're now at their mercy. Will they pay or will they not?

Think about this for a moment. When does your client need you the most? It's before you do the work, not after. So then why are we billing after the fact? Remember supply and demand curves in your Economics 101 class. When demand rises, so does price. To maximize your revenue, you want to have the price discussion when the demand is highest, not when it's the lowest. That's exactly what we do when we bill after the fact. After the fact, the work is already completed. After the fact, the client needs you the least. After the fact, the client has all the control.

To offset that, many accountants simply put in a clause that they will not file their client's tax returns until the invoice is paid in full. Problem solved, right? I always like going into a business transaction with a gun to my head. Feels so safe and gratifying, doesn't it? Talk about setting the tone with your clients. You're basically saying to them that you don't trust them to pay you. I always like going into business with people I don't trust.

Let's also look at it from the perspective of your clients. Coming to their accountant is like going to the dentist, a painful yet necessary evil. They are coming in to get a bunch of tax bills. No one likes to pay taxes. It's not fun. There goes my hard-earned money to the government, they think to themselves. Then we, in our great wisdom, position ourselves right beside that pain by issuing our invoice to them. What are we thinking?

As we sit with our clients at the year-end meeting, we start the "pain" train. I like to call it the Five-Finger Death Punch. It comes from the name of one of my favourite heavy metal bands (inspired from a phrase in a Quentin Tarantino film called *Kill Bill*).

#1 - Here's your personal tax bill (POW!)

#2 - Here's your corporate tax bill (POW!)

#3 - Here's your federal sales tax bill (POW!)

#4 - Here's your provincial (or state) sales tax bill (POW!)

#5 - And to finish you off…here's my bill (POW!)

Knockout blow!

Quentin Tarantino would be proud. That was definitely a *Kill Bill.*

And we wonder why clients don't like going to see their accountants.

Sin #4 – Discounting

Our next sin comes as a so-called solution to the problem of the billing-after-the-fact sin. Someone in their wisdom came up with this brilliant idea. How do we avoid the billing after the fact problem…hmmm…I know, let's show a discount on our bills. No more Five-Finger Death Punch or *Kill Bill*. Problem solved! The client will be happy, right? No, no, no, this is not going to be pretty.

Discounting is like a drug. What seems like a quick fix and gives some instant relief soon becomes an addiction and a downward spiral that becomes difficult, if not impossible, to break. What you thought was the greatest thing on earth becomes your worst nightmare. Let's see what's in store for us if we start down this nightmare path.

First off, discounting your invoices undermines your credibility. We take our proud and noble profession and basically crush our standing in the eyes of our client. What we thought was a kind gesture to make the client feel less pain, through the Five-Finger Death Punch problem, turns around to bite us. Discounting really says one of two things to our clients.

1) That our billable hour rate (how your track our WIP) is really too high for the value they're receiving, so we need to discount the invoice to bring it in alignment.

If we don't discount in the future, they're going to question if they're getting ripped off. Credibility crushed.

2) We took too long on the file. We weren't efficient, and we need to recognize that by discounting our bill to be in alignment with the actual value our client has received. Basically we're telling them we're incompetent, and again, if they don't see a discount in the following year, they're going to question if they're getting ripped off. Crush, crush, crush goes the credibility.

And so starts the vicious cycle.

I remember as a student seeing one of the partners in our firm discounting almost every single invoice that he issued. I didn't realize at the time that I was watching an addiction happening before my eyes. I couldn't put my finger on it then, but I knew it didn't feel right. He would tell me his clients loved seeing the discount (and it made him feel better about issuing his invoices) but the side effects were killing his practice. Today, I can clearly see and explain the side effects of this type of addiction when I'm working with new accounting firm clients. As I'll show you later on, there's a simple solution to this problem that doesn't take a 12-Step Program to recover from.

Sin #5 – Accepting Shitty Clients

When accounting practices rely on compliance filings, they require more and more files to maintain their revenue levels. Downward pressure on pricing accelerates through increases in efficiencies and as such leads to even more returns. Round and round we go, creating our own problem. This need for more files causes our next sin: accepting shitty clients.

This one continually amazes me as I work with my accounting firm clients. It doesn't matter where they're from, accountants just can't let go of clients. Like a bad relationship, they stay connected to clients who really shouldn't be clients as the fear of being without them overtakes their sensibilities. For the outside observer it is easy to see what's happening, but for the one in the relationship it's a much different story.

Who you stop working with is just as important as who you continue working with. Unfortunately for most accountants, they can't see this, because their hand is forced through the business model they've been trapped in. Again, through years of conditioning, they've been trained to accept that the client is always right and the thought of firing someone is just not acceptable. It really is a sad state of affairs, for everyone involved.

The types of shitty clients vary from firm to firm, but generally they fall into three categories—messy files, low pricing, and bad attitude. Each one of these takes value away from the value of an accounting practice. As ironic as it may be, your volume of clients can actually be causing untold damage to your practice.

#1 - Messy files

You know this one all too well. When we were accounting students, we dreaded getting this file from the partner in charge. It was always a shit show. Chasing for missing information, incoherent rationale, and lack of basic bookkeeping skills made these files a nightmare. The worst part was the WIP overruns that you knew were coming and the stress you'd get from the partner when it inevitably happened.

I remember getting these "shit files" every year as an articling student. Again, deep down I knew something was wrong, but I did as I was told and went through the pain of working through the mess. My fellow staff members would giggle under their breath, as the partner in charge assigned me "that" file. I would grin and bear it, going through the pain as a good accountant would. It's like we were chanting like cult members, "More billable hours, more billable hours, more billable hours!"

#2 – Low Pricing

This one drives me nuts. After years and years of schooling and articling to become professional accountants, why oh why do we accept these clients? Whether the client has been with the firm for a long time or if they're a new client, it still boggles my mind why accountants keep them. Again, through the workings of the traditional business model, they remain clients to help the accountant maintain their revenue levels. What seems to be helping actually takes away from the firm.

An interesting thing happens when we accept price-sensitive clients into our practices. It attracts more price-sensitive clients. The law of attraction isn't just an "out there" spiritual concept; it's a physical fact. Scientist have proven it, social psychologists have proven it, and when you look at accounting firm client inventories…yes, even accountants have proven it. Birds of a feather flock together. Talk about adding fuel to a fire. First you have the dynamics of the value curve, and now we've thrown in the "law of attraction" to accelerate the problem. Yikes.

#3 – Bad Attitude

Flipping to the other side of the scale leads us to probably the worst offender, the bad attitude client. This one disguises themselves as a high-price client and maybe even a clean-file client, but to interact with them is poison. The bad-attitude client takes on numerous sub-forms such as:

- Pays late
- Is abrasive with partners and staff

- Is overly demanding
- Always questions your advice
- Goes to other accountants for second opinions
- Questions your fees every year

The list goes on and on. For me, it gets tiring just writing this, never mind living through it again. A quick scan of an accountant's client inventory will reveal these bad eggs in the batch.

My father used to call these types of people "life suckers". You know the ones I'm talking about. Just being in their presence reduces your own energy levels. Some people give energy while others take it away. These bad-attitude clients always take. As kids we were taught to surround ourselves with people who treat you nice, yet here accountants are accepting just the opposite.

Again, it's like being in a bad relationship. It's not until a close friend or family member points out what's happening that the abused person sees clearly. I'm being that friend. Take a look at your client relationships and ask yourself if they are healthy or dysfunctional. A quick review of an accountant's client list reveals a number of relationships that have just got to go.

Sin #6 – Accepting That Tax Time Sucks

One of the worst sins of the traditional business model is accepting that tax time just has to suck. Again, I can't help but to compare this to a bad relationship. Human psychology is an interesting thing, and no part is more interesting or dysfunctional than that of the accountant's acceptance of shitty working conditions. I get it. I was conditioned the same way. It's just what accountants do, right?

When the rest of North Americans are coming out of their homes to enjoy the spring weather, accountants are locked up at their desks, cranking away the hours to complete their client's tax-filing deadlines. What's even more odd is the fact that many accountants wear the crazy hours they work like a badge of honour. Get a group of accountants together, and eventually the conversation gets into a pissing match over who works the most hours in a day. I've often considered getting tee shirts made up that say "I'm so busy" on the front and "because I'm an accountant" on the back.

This acceptance of the status quo (this badge of honour) that work simply sucks around tax time should do the opposite. It should make you mad as hell, because it is hell. Accountants spend years and years of schooling and sacrifice to end up getting chained to a desk for the rest of their life? Come on, really? I thought we were smarter than this. Accountants are very intelligent people. We have to be to pass our accounting exams and become professionals. Why do we accept that our lives must simply suck during tax time? Can't we find a better solution?

Accepting that tax time sucks keeps accountants stuck and repressed. It takes away their power of choice. In a free and democratic society, people have the power to choose. Accountants have consciously given that freedom away to the status quo of the traditional business model. This release of choice keeps accountants from growing personally and professionally. Instead of questioning and looking for solutions, they stay in a life of misery and ultimately become bitter and angry at life. I've met enough accountants in their twilight years to see the long-term effects of this twisted mindset. They are not happy people.

Sin #7 – Wasted Time (Dealing with Time)

Our final deadly sin hits at the heart of the traditional business model used by accountants. In a billable hour model, the amount of time that is wasted simply dealing with time itself is mindboggling. As the saying goes, "Life is short, live it to the fullest and don't waste your time." This seems to fall on deaf ears with accountants when it comes to their beloved billable hour. What a waste of the day to be dealing with this precious gift of time when we could be creating so much more value for our clients and ourselves.

From day one, it was drilled into me that the time sheet was the most important tool for the accountant. To track every six minutes of my day (0.1) was the most important thing I should do. Without this tracking and recording of what I was doing every minute of every day, the entire business would collapse on itself. Armageddon would ensue, and life as I knew it would no longer exist. To add more stress to the mix (if that was possible), I had to make sure all my chargeable hours within each day were maximized. Too much admin time would simply just not do. I mean, heaven forbid I actually work on my business to improve it. We need billable hours, dammit!

From this Holy Grail of tracking our days comes the most precious thing of all, invoicing this "time" to our clients. I can't begin to imagine how many hours of my life I spent deliberating and agonizing over how much of this precious time should be ultimately billed to my clients. How much time was research I should just "eat" vs. time that was purely billable to the client? How much did I charge them last year? How much more time did I spend this year, and was it my fault or the client's fault? Who should pay for this?

The worst part was worrying about how it would affect the client relationship. Oh shit, this year's WIP is higher than last year. Can I bill it? If I do, will the client get upset? What to do, what to do? If I don't bill it, my partners will give me grief (or I'll give myself grief). I can't seem to win on this one. What if I have less time recorded this year vs. last year? Do I drop the bill or take a blessed premium? If I drop it, I'll never be able to bring it back up again. If I take the premium, will I feel guilty, like I'm cheating the client? What does my professional code of ethics say? The list goes on and on.

Then comes the wasted time spent chasing those clients who don't pay their bills right away. Chasing the blessed A/R list. Accountants who have had to take a client to small claims court know how much time that takes up. Nothing is quite so aggravating as chasing to get paid for work you've already done, especially work done during busy season. For those accountants with bills to pay, staff to keep employed, and capital improvements to make, nothing is worse than have an outstanding A/R list.

The most insane part of the billable hour model is the amount of time spent analyzing the time we've tracked! Nothing is more mind-numbing than analyzing overly complex reporting that comes from WIP tracking software. Unutilized WIP, WIP write-off %, recovery time, and projected bill-out rates...the list goes on and on. I remember staring at a partnership analysis report once, and I swear it looked like a science project.

I had a conversation with a partner in a well-established firm in my hometown of Victoria, BC. He was telling me about the amount of work he had just done to transition his firm to a new time-billing software. He was almost bragging that he'd spent over 100 hours (personally) to research and implement this new time-billing software. Think about this for a second. My guess was his charge-out rate was around $400/hour at the time he did this. Basically, if you'd like to keep your billable-hour model intact, he spent over $40,000 in lost revenue to implement software to track his time. I wonder what he (and his partners) thought about his WIP recovery after looking at his time report on that project? Barf.

Ultimately, imagine what you would and could do with all the time that is spent dealing with time. Take a vacation? Spend time with your children? Or perhaps create even more value for your clients and accounting practice? The possibilities are endless, but you can't use what you don't have. Wasting time dealing with time not only doesn't make sense, it's a tragedy to the most precious gift you have—your time here on earth.

CHAPTER 3: Consequences of the Traditional Model

Now that we've covered all of the seven deadly sins, let's turn our attention to the consequences of these sins. All actions have a reaction, and so do all choices have their consequences. Accountants have chosen to stick with the traditional business model. They have chosen to stick with the status quo, and this choice has a ripple effect that touches every aspect of their business and their life. We'll start with the first victim impacted by this choice, the most obvious: you, the professional.

The Professional

The human body is a precious thing. It is also one of the most sophisticated pieces of technology we have on the planet. Even our biggest supercomputers can't touch the processing power of the human body. It's pumping blood throughout our limbs, cells are dividing and fighting off bacteria, and at the same time the mind is processing literally thousands of thoughts every minute. Take a moment to just consider how amazing the body is.

Given this incredible gift we have, why do accountants treat it so poorly? The long hours grinding behind a desk take their toll on our bodies. One accountant I know had to undergo back surgery as a result of many years of tax seasons behind a desk. It's not worth it. Life is precious. The body is precious. And so far, it's the only one we've got—until, of course, we can rebuild our bodies like they did with *The Six Million-Dollar Man*, Steve Austin. I just dated myself, again. Yes, for the record, I did have a Steve Austin action figure as a kid. For those of you who don't know what I'm talking about, do a quick Google search and you'll see. Steve was "the dude" back in the day. Check out the *Bionic Woman* as well. She rocked.

What's even worse is the impact the traditional model has on our mental health. Stress causes all sorts of health problems, and the stressors felt by the accountant during busy season, as well as dealing with the billable hour model in general, have a ripple effect that would astonish you. For those new to the profession, the stress and drive in the beginning can be exhilarating, but it eventually takes its toll. Ask any accountant who has been grinding for the last 20 years how they feel. I have yet to meet a happy accountant who's in the twilight of their career.

The impact of the traditional business model goes beyond just the physical and mental well-being of the professional. Their social life is affected as well. How many times have you had to say no to invitations from friends and family during busy season? Anyone missed their children's events as a result of a filing deadline? In my firm, I had a strict "no overtime" policy for just this reason alone. I went through the first part of my career missing these social gatherings, and I was damned if I was going to do it in the second part (I'll get to how I managed that later on).

The other, shall we call it, "soft impact" of the traditional model is with our client interactions. Our high levels of stress and strain during the busy season and with billing pressures can also affect our clients. I'll discuss this in more detail soon, but for now, think about how our clients think about us. In every client meeting I had, the conversation was the same, "Boy, Erik, you must be really busy this time of year, eh?" It has become a universal truth that accountants have no life during the spring. Even worse is the stereotyping that we actually have no lives at all. Our reputation, as number crunchers, with no personality and stuck behind a desk, is one that makes my blood boil. Accountants are highly intelligent professionals who have sacrificed years to hone their craft. We should be our client's #1 trusted advisor, and we need to reclaim that position now more than ever.

The Employee

The next victims of the traditional business model are our poor employees. We know the stresses that we feel as owners of our practices, but what many accountants forget is the amount of stress their employees feel. I used to call it climbing the corporate ladder and pulling it up behind you. Don't lose sight of the impact your business model has on your team. This means looking clearly at what you've built and how it affects everyone involved. Nothing will make your employees feel more like a number than putting them on the assembly line to crank out chargeable hours.

I remember receiving a file from the partner in charge. The first thing he'd go over was the time budget, which is where the first level of stress would hit. "Get it done within this time frame, or else!" was all I heard. We think pressure is a great motivator for performance, but research shows this just isn't the case. Couple this with the pressure to maximize your billable time, and you've got a conflicting message. Nothing will confuse your staff more than pressuring them to maximize their billable time while in the same breath telling them to not charge too much time!

Every business has but one purpose: to create value for its customers. But where is your employee's incentive to find creative solutions when they're under pressure to charge out time? "If it's not billable, then it's a problem", I can still hear my old bosses saying. The focus on the value of the time sheet is off the mark when it comes to creating true value for our clients. This unhealthy focus spills over into the lives of our staff as well.

This pressure also manifests itself in other "non-professional" ways as well. Have you ever "fudged" your time sheet before? Either not recording all the time you worked on a client file (for fear of WIP overruns and grief from the partner in charge) or padding the billable hours to help your bonus? More than once, I've seen senior accountants not delegating work out properly for fear of losing billable hours (and their bonuses). Talk about incentive to do something non-ethical. So much for a proud and noble profession...

Cranking out long overtime hours and the heavy stress loads during tax season is also no longer acceptable to today's workers. Simply dangling the carrot of bonus money or future partnership is no longer sufficient to attract the right people. Today's professional accountant wants more from their career. They want to feel purposeful and rewarded by what they do every day. More importantly, they want a life outside of their career. They want time and freedom, and they aren't willing to sacrifice themselves like the old-school guard used to do. Firms that remain within the old model will soon find themselves unable to attract and retain the talent they need to have a successful accounting practice.

The Firm

Next comes the impact to the firm itself, and we can easily continue where we left off regarding the employees. To attract and retain great talent, today's accounting firm needs to give its employees a higher purpose and the flexibility to live their life on their terms. Firms stuck in the traditional model cannot provide this for their team. As we shall see later on, firms that update their business model will attract the best of the best and will have the ability to create even more value for their clients and their staff. Every time I speak to a group of employees on this subject, it's like looking at a sea of bobble-head dolls. Everyone is nodding in agreement. They don't like the stress of the traditional model, and they want (and deserve) a better way of doing business.

Firms that stick to the traditional model are also doomed to a world of vanilla. I review hundreds of accounting firm websites every month, and the similarities are staggering. Each one sounds exactly like the other. They all say, "We are a full-service accounting firm, we pride ourselves on a high attention to detail, and we customize our services to the needs of our clients...because we care." Sound familiar? How do you stand out in a crowd when everyone looks, sounds, and acts like everyone else? Everyone is vanilla.

Billing by the hour and tracking time have another "wonderful" side effect for the firm (yes, notice the sarcasm yet again). As we know our balance sheet dynamics all too well, let's answer this question:

> What supports all that WIP and A/R on your books?
>
> **Answer:** Capital.

This capital comes in either the form of partnership contributions or other indebtedness (like bank loans). The amount of capital tied up in A/R and WIP can be staggering. This capital is not growing for firms either. Unlike borrowing to buy real estate or investing in an upward-rising stock, the capital used for A/R and WIP requirements is what I call "dead money". When was the last time you saw A/R or WIP appreciate in value? It's almost laughable really.

Lastly is the effect the traditional model has on the valuation of the accounting firm. Like all businesses, one of the main drivers on valuation comes down to cash flow. For the firm with capital locked up in A/R and WIP, and the sporadic peaks and valleys of cash flow from busy tax seasons, it's no wonder most firms are undervalued. Instead of getting a multiple on billings, most firms are getting pennies on the dollar. We'll examine a solution to this problem later on. For now, suffice it to say the traditional firm is just like most accountants; overworked and unvalued.

The Client

Let's take a deeper dive into the effects on our clients. The stress of the traditional model on our clients is brutal. We've already seen the impact the Five-Finger Death Punch has on them and the reflection it has on us in their eyes. Like going to the dentist, coming to see the accountant becomes a necessary evil. Visits are a necessary and painful event. **Stress impact #1.**

Stress impact #2 is purchase fatigue. Ever had a client not call you about some important decision that has implications for your tax-planning strategies? Like say, getting their wills redone without your knowledge beforehand? Never, right? They always call us first…NOT! Ever wonder why this is the case? Why would normally intelligent people not think to call their accountant to be involved in something so critical?

The answer is simple. They do think about calling us, it's just that they're feeling the effects of what I call purchase fatigue. Think about it. Every time they go to give their accountant a call, about anything, they need to make a buying decision.

They're saying to themselves, "Is this problem I have worth calling my accountant, given I'm going to get a bill for the answer?" Or even worse, "I'll get a bill even though I may NOT get an answer!"

When anyone goes to buy anything, they are making a buying decision. "Is the price I'm about to pay worth the value I'm about to receive?" This goes for everything. From a can of pop at the corner store to a dream mansion on the oceanside, behind every economic transaction, a buying decision must first be made. Equally so, every time they think to call they are making a buying decision. And when you think about how much they could use our expertise in their businesses and financial lives, this becomes a great number of decisions to make. Purchase fatigue.

Stress impact #3 – writing a blank cheque. What's truly astonishing to me is how most accountants don't see how negatively this impacts their clients, who they apparently care so much for (as noted on their websites). Don't you like to know how much something is going to cost before you purchase it? Of course you do. Everybody does. So why do our clients have to basically write a blank cheque for our services?

In all fairness, they don't actually write us a blank cheque, because they can ultimately decide to fight us on the year-end invoice if they're really unhappy with the price. However, if they wish to maintain the relationship or avoid the battle of court proceedings, simply paying the bill is the easier route. I always used to ask a new client prospect why they were leaving their existing accountant. I can't count how many times they would answer that it was because of getting surprised on the invoices.

Stress impact #4 – when clients look at their accountant, all they see is cost. Each of the previous stress impacts culminates in this last one; with the necessary evil, purchase fatigue, and writing a blank cheque, clients see us as a cost center vs. a value provider.

Going into the year-end meeting is always the same for clients. They are wondering how much the services are going to cost them this year. They have an idea of what last year's bill was, so they're hoping it's about the same…or better yet, even less (see the discounting trap in Chapter 2). They're always hoping for a lower bill. "I need to keep my accounting costs down" is the mantra.

Cost bad. Revenue good.

Accountant bad. Sales team good.

After speaking and working with accountants from all over the world, I've seen two major themes arise. They feel overworked and undervalued. And it's no wonder they feel undervalued by their clients. It's not an illusion. It's real. Their clients see them as a cost center and not a value center. The client is the victim of this perspective as well. By seeing us in this light, they are unable to extract the incredible value we can provide them. We have the training and we have the skills to give them so much more than just tax returns and compliance filings. And they deserve so much more.

The Family...and friends

One of the saddest consequences of the traditional business model is the effect it has on our family and friends. Long, hard hours, stressful working conditions, and the self-esteem impacts of being undervalued by clients spill out into the professional's social circles. None are impacted more than the professional's first circle: their family.

The accountant's spouse is where the majority of the friction comes. Especially if they aren't in the profession, it becomes incredibly difficult for the spouse to understand why we work the way we do. It's bad enough that we have to put in the long hours of tax season without having additional pressures coming from home. So many relationships fail as a result of mismatched expectations surrounding the accountant's dedication to their career.

What's even worse is the effect it can have on the kids. Missed recitals, school events, sports, and even just simple play time can all be results of the long hours taken up from the drive for billable time. Even when the accountant is home and available, they are normally totally burnt out and unable to play as a result of the work that they've done. Instead of being energized by the work that they do, most accountants are bitter and pissed off at the state of their affairs. I have yet to meet a happy accountant during busy season.

This frustration within the accountant spills over to extended family and friends as well. Missed functions, dinners, and family gatherings are the norm during those days of tax season. When the rest of the family and our friends are starting to enjoy the oncoming of spring, we are locked to our desks, racking up the billable time to make a living. Even if the accountant does make it to the functions, they are not normally a very pleasant person to be around. A stressed-out person is inevitably a grumpy person.

What's even worse is that the accountant's family and friends don't understand what's going on in the accountant's head. They can't comprehend why we're so stressed out. They've never been through a tax season before from our side. They don't get it. I remember getting ready for a show my friends and I were putting on for a tribute band I was playing in called Motley 2 (yes, I did mention I love 80s hair metal, didn't I?) They booked a show in late April. Late April! What the hell were they thinking! That was the last show we did, as the friction between myself and the rest of the band was too much. I had been so busy working that I was mentally and physically unable to give a helping hand to get ready for the show. People just don't understand the pressures we face…but nor should they. Working like an accountant doesn't compute to a normal person.

The Future

Lastly, I'd like to take a moment to consider what consequences the traditional business model has on the future, both the profession's future and your own. What is going to happen to those firms that stay stuck in the old model and don't change with the times? Everyone's head is stuck in the sand thinking everything is okay, but it's not. There's a tsunami coming.

Picture a beach full of accountants. Everyone has ample space to put down their beach towel. Everything's great, right? Then the water starts to recede, and they all start rushing to put their blankets down on this new fresh sand that's been created (by technology-driven efficiencies). Those accountants who understand what's really happening know this isn't good, this isn't good at all. They start to head for higher ground. When the tsunami of the AI and technology wave hits, it's going to decimate the profession. Only those who saw the writing on the wall and went for higher ground are going to survive.

There's an interesting phenomenon that happens with groups of people. It's called "herd mentality". It stems from groups of wild animals that herd together as a survival instinct. Those who stay deep within the herd survive predator attacks, while those on the outside of the herd fall victim. Accountants act the same way. There appears to be safety in numbers, but this isn't always the case, especially in business. It's those businesses owners who break new ground that reap the rewards, not the ones who look and sound just like everyone else. But this is more than just being like everyone else. This is about being wiped out…just like everyone else.

Charles Darwin was right. Survival of a species depends on its ability to adapt to its environment. Those that adapt, thrive. Those that don't, go extinct. The traditional model needs to be updated. Dependence on compliance filings and the billable hour, and a focus on increasing efficiencies, need to be replaced. Who will survive this inevitable tsunami? I'm really hoping it will be you. That's why I wrote this book. That's my hope for you and your future. To not only survive, but to thrive.

That's what the Accountant Success Formula™ did for me and continues to do for those accountants implementing it into their practices.

Before we get into the details of the Accountant Success Formula™, let's make sure you're 100% ready to make this shift. With all change comes the first step, and that first step is your mindset. This next chapter will set the stage for you to make this change. Let's deal with first things first.

CHAPTER 4: First Things First

We've now reviewed the past, present, and future of our proud and noble profession. We've opened our eyes to the seven deadly sins of the traditional model. And finally, we've squarely faced the consequences to not only ourselves but to all those around us of remaining stagnant in the old model. The question now becomes a very simple one. What are you going to do about it?

Life's Too Short...

I have a great saying that I use. I actually live and breathe it every day because I know how true it is. Every time I say it, I get the following responses from accountants everywhere, regardless of where they live in the world. Some nod in agreement. Some giggle nervously. And some simply droop their shoulders down in defeat and surrender while saying, "You're right, Erik." The saying is:

Life's too short…to work like an accountant.

Life is short, and it's precious. It's a gift that none of us should squander. The interesting thing about human nature is that we take life for granted and don't stop often enough to ask ourselves if we're really living life to the fullest. What's equally true is that it normally takes a life-shattering moment to wake us up to this fact and make us do something about it. The death of a close friend or family member, a near-fatal accident, or a life-changing event is normally what it takes to give us the jolt we need to re-evaluate our lives and make a change.

That's exactly what happened to me. I had a serious wake-up call. I'm so grateful that I did, because had I not been jolted awake, I shudder to think of what my life would have looked like today. What sometimes seems like the worst event in your life can actually be, in hindsight, the best thing that has ever happened to you. I'm grateful for having gone through it, but at the same time would never wish it on anyone.

It was the collapse of my first partnership; I thought I had lost everything. I had over 18 years of hard work and recognition disappear overnight. I was devastated. This seemingly brutal tragedy actually turned out to be the biggest blessing of my professional career. I decided to pick up the pieces and open my own accounting firm, yet this time I was determined to do things differently.

I asked myself repeatedly, "Why?" Why was I under the illusion that if I only worked harder, the payoff would finally come, when in reality, the days were only getting longer and the payoff was getting shorter? With the aftershock of the collapse of my partnership, I felt like I had woken up for the first time, and I saw the insanity of it all. There had to be a better way.

I decided to study some of the most powerful thought leaders in business and rethink the current model used by most accounting firms. From my research and through many years of experimentation, I developed an updated business model for my new practice. It not only tripled my revenues, it allowed me to work with only the best clients, and to have far more time and freedom than I had ever imagined.

We don't have to blindly follow what our mentors and predecessors told us to do. We don't have to work insane hours to make the money we want and to get rewarded for our years of study and sacrifice. We just have to be willing to consider a new way of doing business. The question for you is, "Have you had enough of the old model?" Are you willing to find a better way? You don't have to go through a life-shattering event before you make your move. It can be done voluntarily, before the extreme pain and suffering that most have to go through to make a change.

Inner Game

Inevitably every single accountant that I've worked with has to first deal with their "inner game". Shifting your mindset to be open to a new way of business is not as easy as it sounds for many of us. And it's no wonder why. We've been brainwashed into following the status quo. Years and years of conditioning are not easily changed overnight. It can be a difficult process for some. Falling back into old habits and patterns is normal. A reconditioning period is required. New habits take time, so have patience and be persistent. Stay the course long enough, and eventually new behaviours will take hold and replace those that are no longer serving you.

It's also amazing to me the power fear has to keep us from evolving and growing as human beings. Nothing like fear to keep you stuck exactly where you are, regardless of how bad it is. I love this acronym for fear:

False
Evidence
Appearing
Real

The fear of the unknown can easily overpower the pain and suffering of the known. Crazy, isn't it? Ever tried talking a friend out of a bad relationship only to have them say they're too scared to leave, regardless of how bad it is? "What if I don't find someone else and I live the rest of my life alone?" they say. People get comfortable in their misery. It's the comfort of the known vs. the fear of the unknown. The truth of the matter is that nothing will change in your life until you do something about it. The question again is, are you willing to do something?

Ultimately, it comes down to self-worth. Are you worth it? Do you deserve better in your career and your life, or are you okay with living life like a typical accountant? Let me answer this one for you. You are worth it. You've spent so many years and sacrifice to become a professional accountant that it's time you reap the rewards of all your hard work. You are worth it. I know that. But that's not going to help until you know that and claim it for yourself.

Entrepreneur?

Something that continues to amaze me is how accountants forget that they are in business. We advise and provide all these consulting services to our own business clients yet, somehow, we become immune to our own advice. It's like a blind spot for accountants. We're different, we think to ourselves, we're professionals, we're not like other businesses. Oh really?

Michael Gerber, co-author of *The E-Myth Accountant*, uses a great saying that I re-quote all the time. He says, "Accounting firms are run by technicians having an entrepreneurial seizure." How true this is. We've gone through hundreds, if not thousands, of hours of technical training to become professional accountants, yet it's come with a huge blind spot—how to run our own businesses. We're not in a bubble, immune from market shifts and consumer preferences. We're in business, and we need to adapt just like anyone else.

Think about this for a moment. You joined or started your firm for a reason, didn't you? Can you remember what that reason was? Do you live it every day? When working with my one-on-one coaching clients, I have them go back to the beginning and clearly define their "Why". Specifically, why they are in business. From this answer flow all decisions to ensure that strategically they are keeping themselves in alignment with that "Why".

Everyone's "Why" is different, but there are some universally consistent themes such as:

- Make a great living.
- Be respected.
- Provide for their family.
- Have job security.
- Be able to save up for retirement.

What is truly shocking is the lack of clarity most accountants have with their own exit strategy. Would you not want to be able to maximize the value of your practice so that when you go to retire you could sell it for a great price? Of course you would. Then why aren't they building it to do just that? Take some time to get clear on your why (from start to finish) for your practice, and you'll be setting the stage for you to act and make the right decisions to make it all happen.

Follow the Lemmings!

I have this picture in my mind of accountants as a group of lemmings, blindly following each other off a cliff into the abyss. It's what happens in a herd mentality. People are like animals and feel safety in numbers. There is a natural tendency to follow the crowd. It feels safe. It feels right. It feels comfortable.

As accountants, we have been trained to be conservative. It's been drilled into us from day one. That's why our clients trust us so much, right? But this attractive and valuable trait becomes a boomerang when it comes to our decisions as a business owner. "Stay the course and don't rock the boat", we chant. All the other accountants are going this way…follow, follow, follow. What happens when everyone is doing the same thing? Nobody stands out!

One of the greatest investors of all time, Warren Buffet, knows the herd mentality incredibly well, and he has used it to his advantage to amass incredible wealth. He has a simple and yet counterintuitive investing policy. When everyone is selling off, he buys. When everyone is buying, he's selling. It's genius. He knows that individuals are smart, but when groups of people herd they become like lemmings walking off a cliff. He's more than happy to make sure he takes some of the wealth that they're carrying off their hands before they take the final plunge into the abyss.

Are You Ready?

Let's go back to our question at the beginning of this chapter:

What are you going to do about all this?

You have a choice. Are you ready to do something different and change the trajectory of your career and your life? All change starts with a realization that there is a problem and that something new is required. From there, you find that something new and then you take action. A great idea is worthless unless it is followed up by focused action to make that new idea a reality.

My wish for you is that you reap the rewards of all your years of hard work and sacrifice to become a professional accountant. You deserve it. I know you do. I went through hell and back myself to finally get the rewards. It's now time for you. It's yours for the taking. All you need to do now is decide you're going to do something, anything, to stop the insanity of it all. You're about to step into a new world. You're going to get the respect you deserve. The money you deserve. The time and freedom you deserve.

If you've recognized the problem, have made a choice that it needs to change, and are now willing to take action, then you're ready to go onto the next chapter. If however, you're not completely convinced, or you're content with the way things are in your practice, then stop reading and go back to doing what you've always done. Continue to follow the herd and stay in your safe place. Change is not easy, especially if you've been programed and conditioned for years (and for some of you, even decades) to follow the status quo. This formula I'm about to share is for those who are sick and tired of the old model and are ready to embrace a new way of doing business. It's for those who realize the traditional model is no longer a fit for themselves or their clients. It's for those who want to build an incredibly successful accounting practice. It's for those who want to build a truly successful life.

It's for you.

CHAPTER 5: New Beginnings – The Accountant Success Formula™

Outline

This chapter is broken into three sections. In the first section, I'll cover the big picture and walk through the three stages of the business lifecycle. You naturally end up talking to your clients about this when they come to you for advice, but rarely have I seen accountants actually apply it to their own businesses.

The second section is an outline of the four critical questions you will want to have clear answers for as you build your new business model. These simple, yet powerful questions are addressed throughout the Accountant Success Formula™ and will form the backbone for your new world.

In the third section, we will outline the five components of the Accountant Success Formula™ (or as we like to call it, the ASF 5). I recommend all my coaching clients have a copy of the ASF 5 sitting in a visible place, so they can refer back to it as a constant reminder throughout their working day. I find the easiest way is to simply print it out and stick to the wall near your desk (yes, I know it sounds old school, but it works). Let's get started.

SECTION 1 – Business Lifecycle

I remember when I was offered partnership in my first firm. The senior partner sat me down and went through the partnership agreement with me. One thing stood out for me right away as I attempted to digest the document. It was basically broken down into three parts. It detailed the mechanics of what would happen as the partnership started (ENTRY), how profits would be allocated as we operated (DURING), and how the partnership would be dissolved based on a number of different scenarios (EXIT).

This simple three-stage outline (ENTRY, DURING, EXIT) makes up the lifecycle of any business. It served me well for over 26 years as I provided advisory services inside my accounting practice. It continues to work today as I share it with my accounting firm coaching clients. It provides clarity and forces us to look at what is expected (or at least makes us think of it) as we design our businesses to suit our lives.

When you start to look at what your accounting practice will go through during these stages, many questions will start to arise. In addition, it will make you become more purposeful in what you're doing. Purpose is everything when it comes to action. Without a clear purpose, action becomes wasted effort. It becomes simply doing something for the sake of doing something!

Let's quickly look at the three stages to paint a picture of what your optimal business lifecycle could look like. From there, we'll look at the four critical questions to be answered, and then we'll use the ASF 5 as our action steps to make it a reality.

Entry

Picture having a crystal-clear vision for your practice and knowing exactly what you're going to build and why. A clear vision and purpose makes life so much easier than simply the "build it and they will come" mentality. I'll dive into the four questions in greater detail next, but for now, think about the purpose of your practice. What is your practice for? Why did you go into public practice in the first place? Write down the reasons. We'll be expanding on this later on.

During

As you're working in your practice, what would you like to experience? For many accountants, the following list is a dream:

- Reduced stress
- Increased earnings
- Working with great clients who appreciate the value you provide and are happy and willing to pay you incredibly well
- Attracting great employees
- Having consistent and predictable cash flow to make business decisions
- Having free time throughout each month of the year

After the implosion of my first partnership, this list was not only my dream, but my driving force. I was determined to make these things happen, and I did. Write down what a perfect day would look like in your accounting practice. Picture doing just the parts you love, and exclude all those tasks you despise. This is the goal we are going to move towards.

Exit

As you leave your accounting practice, how does the following sound?

- High valuation
- Easily finding a buyer or buyers
- Having multiple offers on your practice
- Having no purchase-price-adjustment clause based on client retention

- Making a clean transition to the new owner (you're not required to stay on)

This is the exit I experienced in my practice. Was it luck? No, it wasn't. I had entered the practice on purpose, ran it to provide me a great lifestyle while I was working in it, and built it for an easy and profitable exit. Entry, During & Exit are the three stages every business goes through. The real question is: Are you going to be the one driving those stages, or are you going to let those stages drive you? Write down what your exit will look like for you in the future, and make a decision to make it happen.

SECTION 2 – Your Four Questions

Want better answers? Ask better questions. And what's equally true is that it's the simple ideas that are most effective in life. If you have to explain a question in great detail, you've missed the mark. Keep it simple. This includes the questions to ask yourself about your accounting practice as well. Get ready to do some work here, as this is the critical foundation you're going to build upon.

Why

The first question is **Why**. Why are you doing what you're doing? The answer may seem incredibly simple, yet when you invest a little time actually writing out the answers, many things will become clear. Write them out in bullet form right now. For many accountants, the answers look something like this:

- To make money to live
- To support my family
- To be respected as a professional
- I went to school to do this
- I find it stimulating and challenging
- I want to make $x amount per year (be specific)
- To provide me a stable retirement
- I want to experience the flexibility and freedom of running my own business

Once you clearly understand your **Why**, you can then purposefully build your practice to support it. Are you making the income you want? Are you getting the respect you deserve? Do you have the freedom you were seeking? Write it all down.

Who

The next question is **Who**. Who are you going to serve in your accounting practice? Too many accountants make the mistake of attempting to serve everyone. They tell the market, "We are a full-service accounting practice." If you want to remain bland, sounding like everyone else, then serve everyone. If you're good at everything, then you're great at nothing. For now, let's start the niching process and see if we can get a capture of whom you're going to serve.

Write out the answers to these questions:

- Who do you love to work with the most?
- When working with these people, do you perform at your best?
- Why do you love working with them?
- What are the specific qualities of these clients?
- More importantly, are there any clients you dislike working with?
- When you work with these people, do you perform at your worst?
- Why do you dislike working with them?
- What are the specific qualities of these clients?

Pay equal time and attention to the ones you don't like working with. My mentor Paul Dunn (co-author of the book and CEO of the global impact movement B1G1) would argue that the clients you don't like working with are even more important to identify. He has a wonderful acronym he shared with me: **SIWSNT**. It stands for:

Success
Is

What (and Who) you
Say
No
To

The market will pay you a premium on your services based on whom you don't serve and what you don't do. Make sure you've got a clear picture in your mind of those clients you don't want to work with, as it is incredibly valuable.

What

Next is **What**. As with the why question, it is just as important to determine what services you're going to provide as what you going to provide. For this question, answer the following:

- What services do you love to provide?
- What services are you great at delivering?
- What services do your clients value the most?
- What services do you hate to provide?
- What services do you fall short at delivering?
- What services do your clients value the least?

There are many things accountants "can" do, but very few things they should do. Just because we're in public practice doesn't mean we should be doing everything for everybody. Again, if you do everything, you're great at nothing. Anyone with experience asking their client's lawyer to prepare a corporate reorganization or estate freeze will know that some lawyers should not be doing this work. I used to cringe when I asked a lawyer if they did reorgs and they would respond, oh yes, we "can" do that. I didn't ask if they could do that, I asked if they did do that. I "could" do brain surgery, but do you want me to practice it on you? I didn't think so.

How

Finally, once you've become clear on your **Why**, and have identified **Who** and **What** services you are going to provide (and again, more importantly, who you won't be serving and what you won't be doing— **SIWSNT**), you then need to determine **How** you're going to deliver it all. This is the final piece of the puzzle, and regardless of the work you've done on the first three questions, if you don't get this one right, it will all go to hell.

Some of the answers you need to nail down are:

- Will I provide this solo, or will I build a team around me?
    - If yes, then how much interaction do I provide vs. my team?

- How will I interact with my clients?
    - Touch points?
    - Example: face-to-face or remotely?

- How will I provide the deliverables in my practice?
- How will I charge and capture the value I'm providing my clients?

The **How** is the icing on the cake. It is the final piece to ensure your practice is going to provide you the lifestyle and income flow you truly want and deserve. It doesn't matter the amount of great ideas you have if you don't deliver them. It all comes down to the execution of those ideas. Action, "The **How**", is the most important. As we will see later on in the chapter, the **How** can make or break your practice.

In the final section, we will dive into the five components of the Accountant Success Formula™ (the ASF 5). Note that each section will address one or more of your four questions. The **Why, Who, What,** and **How** all form the backbone of your practice. As such, it is critical that your new business model incorporates the answers to these questions.

SECTION 3 – The ASF 5

ASF 1 – Positioning (Why)

In business, positioning is everything. It defines what your company stands for and more importantly what it doesn't stand for. It defines whom you work with and whom you don't. It defines what price point and level of service you're providing in relation to your competitors. It defines you.

Where are you positioning your accounting practice?

Before you answer that, let's refer back to Ric's Value Curve:

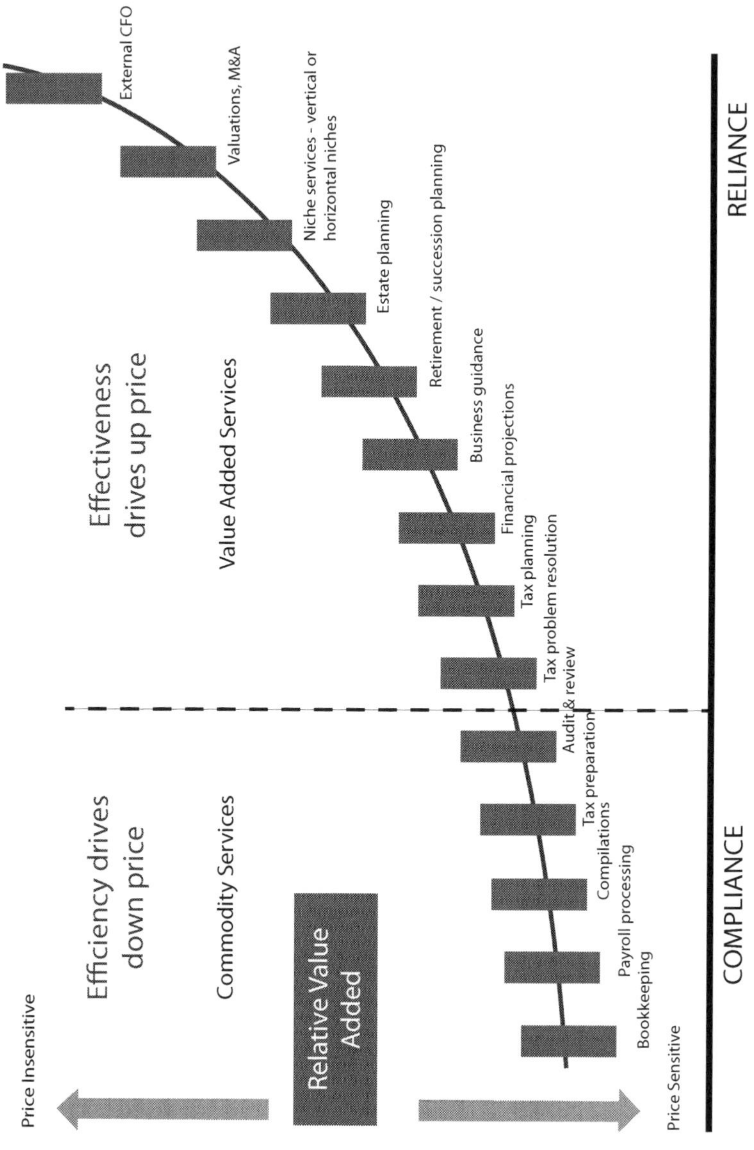
Price Insensitive
Price Sensitive
Relative Value Added
Efficiency drives down price
Commodity Services
Effectiveness drives up price
Value Added Services
Bookkeeping
Payroll processing
Compilations
Tax preparation
Audit & review
Tax problem resolution
Tax planning
Financial projections
Business guidance
Retirement / succession planning
Estate planning
Niche services - vertical or horizontal niches
Valuations, M&A
External CFO
COMPLIANCE
RELIANCE

We know that services performed at the left side of the curve are those that are considered less valuable in the eyes of your clients. We also know that the only way to make your margins on that type of work is to increase your efficiencies (you need to do more files as each one is at a lower price point). In economics, increase in efficiency puts downward pressure on price. We also know that advances in technology are speeding up that efficiency train.

We've got a perfect storm. If you stay at this point on the curve, you'll have to continually do more work for less money. Arguably, you may even be out of business if and when artificial intelligence starts doing all these tasks on the left-hand side of the curve automatically. Yikes! Is this why you went to school for so many years to become a professional accountant? To be stuck in a model that dooms you to do more, for less money, and all the while pointing you towards eventual extinction? I think not!

The positioning you want to be taking is that of services provided on the right side of the curve. These services have upward pressure on price, because your clients value these services so much more. These services are effective in providing the real value your clients want. You can charge higher prices, and your clients will gladly pay for them (especially the farther right you go on the curve).

Herein lies the positioning I share with all my coaching clients. Position yourself to the farthest possible spot on the curve. Go to the highest value spot you can, the farthest away from the train-wreck of lower-value compliance services. Position yourself as your client's CFO, or as I sometimes like to call it, their financial quarterback. I'll get more into how to sell this positioning to your clients later on in ASF 3 – Sales, but for now, make a decision to capture the best price you can by delivering the highest value possible to your clients. This clears up the compliance problem we discussed earlier and gives you a route to traverse that danger.

Next comes the billable hour trap. When you've positioned yourself to the right side of the Value Curve, make sure you've captured the value you're truly providing. That value cannot be captured through a billable hour model. It can only be captured through a value-pricing model. Throw away your time sheets and bill what you're worth. I'll walk you through exactly how to do that in ASF 4 - Professional Service Agreements.

What does value pricing and throwing out time sheets have to do with positioning, you may be asking yourself? Has Erik just gone on a tangent? Was he distracted by some heavy metal music blaring in the background as he was writing this section? What is he thinking? Seriously…WTF?

Throwing away the timesheet is positioning. It could arguably be the best positioning you can take. It will set you free, and it will set you apart from everyone else in the market. I show all my coaching clients how to openly announce this fact to their referral network and throughout their marketing materials. It is a breath of fresh air for clients. When you couple this with services on the right side of the Value Curve, you have a recipe for something amazing.

Positioning is not only your starting point; it is a theme that permeates throughout the remaining four components of the Accountant Success Formula™. Once you've decided your positioning, clarity arises. You'll no longer question which way to go when faced with choices. You'll clearly see what needs to be done to fulfill your positioning and you'll be able to take immediate action.

Resist the urge to copy everyone else. Exceptional money is made on the fringes of a market. You want to be able to stand out against a backdrop of vanilla firms touting their "full-service" model. Stop doing what everyone else is doing—pick a lane and stick to it. This means clearly defining not only who you're going to work with and what you're going to do, but more importantly who you're not going to work with and what services you're not going to offer.

And speaking of who…let's get into that right now.

ASF 2 – Inventory (Who)

Accountants complain (but mostly brag) about how they're so extremely busy all the time. I talk to hundreds of accountants every month, and when I ask them how they're doing, the answer is always the same, "I'm sooooooo busy." Interestingly enough, when I then say, "You must be making a killing then", all I hear are crickets. They stare at me with that deer-in-the-headlights look. Hmmm…then why are they working so much? One look at their client inventory, and the answer becomes clear. They are spending way too much time on "low-hanging fruit", so to speak.

It amazes me how many accountants don't take their own advice. They advise their retail clients to take regular inventory, yet they won't even take a few minutes to look at their own. Yes, your clients are your inventory, just like a retail business's products are. And just like in any other business, if you're not taking stock, you're fooling yourself about the financial health of your accounting practice. Remember the saying, "A bad apple will spoil the bunch"? Same thing applies to your clients.

The Pareto Principle also comes into play here in a big way. The Pareto Principle (also known as the 80/20 rule) states that, for many events, roughly 80% of the effects come from 20%

of the causes. This principle applies equally to an accounting firm's performance when you look at its client inventory. Simply put, 80% of your revenues come from the top 20% of clients. What's even more shocking is when you apply this same principle to the net profits of an accounting practice. Literally 150% of the net profits come from 20% of the top clients, while a negative 50% (yes, I said negative) is taken by your bottom 80%. If you were to simply get rid of your bottom 80% (along with the corresponding cost drivers), and not even add any extra work, you'd instantly make 50% more money every year.

The first thing required of you is to simply do an inventory count. Anyone who's gone through an audit file knows the importance of the inventory count. This exercise, however, will not be anywhere near as painful as attending one of your clients' inventory counts, I promise. It will be one of the most beneficial exercises you will ever do in your practice. Plus, you'll want to continually revisit your inventory to make sure it's clean and, more importantly, keeping you incredibly profitable.

A simple spreadsheet is all you need. List all your clients down the left-hand side, and then categorize them into four lists along the top. You'll end up having columns A, B, C, and X. Rank your clients by quality, revenue source, and fit into your positioning. In each column, enter the revenue from each client according to where they fit. In the X column, enter those clients you know need to go immediately, regardless of revenue levels. These are those bad apples that are spoiling your batch.

Client Name	A	B	C	X
ACB Corp	$12,000			
Big Profit Corp		$ 6,000		
Jerk Corp				$ 3,000
Plenty-O-Fun Inc.			$ 3,000	
Dog Walker Inc.			$ 1,500	
TOTALS	**$12,000**	**$ 6,000**	**$ 4,500**	**$ 3,000**

Accountants very often make the critical mistake of thinking that the more clients they have, the better. Wrong. Having more bad apples is simply having more of a bad thing. Client quality is more important than client quantity. One quick look at your inventory, and you'll see those bad apples and want to get rid of them immediately (these are represented by the X column). C clients are clients who take up a large amount of your time and energy with less return that those great A & B clients. C-level clients are still nice apples in your bunch, but they're not as shiny and tasty as the A's & B's. Ultimately, if you want to have a great, profitable practice, you want to reduce the number of C's as well.

Think of your accounting practice like an airplane. You've only got so many seats on a plane. These seats are broken up into first class, business class, and economy class. These are your A, B, and C clients. X clients shouldn't even be on your plane, so don't give them a seat. Picture for a moment what your practice would look like if you increased the number of seats in your first-class cabin of your airplane? You'd have to reduce the number of seats elsewhere, right? Naturally, you'd reduce the number of economy-class seats and then, viola: you'd be more profitable. You have the same number of seats, but now you've got more revenue overall, since you charge more for the first-class seats.

This is where most accountants go running away, screaming in terror, "I can't let clients go! I need the revenue!" The amount of time and effort spent on low-value clients (C & X) can be mind-blowing. It's not our fault, however—we've been conditioned to think this way. I get it. We've already faced the facts that we've been conditioned and this conditioning no longer serves us, so now it's time to do something different. It's time to start working smarter and not harder in our practices.

Let's do some simple math to model out what I'm talking about. Take an example of an accountant looking to generate $600,000 in annual billings. They start by doing a few friends' and family members' personal tax returns, and they do them for say, $150 each. At this rate, they would need 4,000 clients to reach $600K (4,000 x $150). Simple math. Time to get smarter—let's double our prices to $300. That still means they need 2,000 clients to reach $600K (2,000 x $300). You get where I'm going with this now. Let's look at the following table for five ways to get to $600K:

# Clients	$ Price	$ Revenue
4,000	$ 150	$ 600,000
2,000	$ 300	$ 600,000
200	$ 3,000	$ 600,000
100	$ 6,000	$ 600,000
50	$12,000	$ 600,000

Managing client inventory is extremely critical to the success of any accounting practice. The clients should align with the positioning of the firm, the price point, and the services provided. What's even more important is that the inventory should be constantly reviewed and managed. The goal is to ensure that the bad apples (X clients) are removed to avoid spoiling the bunch, and that you're always looking to decrease the number of C-class seats while increasing the A- & B-class seats.

ASF 3 – Sales (What)

The next component of the ASF 5 is sales. But before we go any further, let's be brutally honest with ourselves for a moment:

Accountants suck at sales.

To be fair, it's not our fault. We were never properly trained on how to sell, which is crazy when you think about it. Nothing in business happens until someone sells something to a customer or a client. It would seem logical then that this would be the FIRST thing one should learn before they go into business, right?

WRONG!

For some reason, our collective viewpoint on sales is that it's unprofessional. It's like "sell" is a four-letter word to accountants. The minute I bring up selling, I can see visions of sleazy used-car salesmen running through the mind of an accountant.

To be successful in business, however, you need to sell. A business can't survive without sales. That's why a business exists in the first place, to sell something! The art of selling is a massive topic just on its own. Perform a quick web search, and you'll find unlimited experts out there selling you programs on how to sell. To keep things really simple, though, just ask one question:

What do accountants sell?

Anyone? Anyone?

Bueller...
Bueller...
Bueller...

Sorry, I couldn't help myself. *Ferris Bueller's Day Off* is one of my wife's favourite movies of all time (right behind). Anyways, I digress.

Seriously though, what do accountants sell?

- Tax returns?
- Financial statements?
- Advisory services?

It's actually none of the above.

The only thing ANYONE sells is good feelings, plain and simple.

There's an old marketing saying: people don't buy drills; they buy the anticipation of holes. People buy good feelings. We are either taking away some pain or adding some pleasure to their lives. Every single good or service is simply a vehicle for good feelings. This is where accountants get everything mixed up. When accountants sell, they focus solely on the stuff they provide, not the good feelings their clients will feel as a result of the services. I can hear the laundry list of "stuff" they will take care of during a sales conversation: "We will take care of your personal taxes, corporate taxes, this filing, that filing, blah, blah, blah." Better yet, they even quote every technical filing form along the way. That's a great way to make your clients fall asleep.

The primary problem with this backwards point of view is that the accountant confuses the value the client receives with the amount of stuff the accountant does. In other words, the accountant somehow thinks the amount of hours spent on the client's file equals the value the client actually receives. The value the client receives is only based on the amount of pain or pleasure they experience as a result of the service, not the amount of hours the accountant puts in. Why oh why then, do we still think that a billable hour model is the way to capture the true value we provide our clients?

Value is like beauty; it's in the eye of the beholder. What is valuable (or beautiful) to one person may not be as valuable (or beautiful) to another. The value received by one person will naturally not be the same as another. This is exactly why you need to get to know your client before you quote the price. Investing that extra time at the front end of the engagement to truly understand where your client's pain points are is critical to capturing the value you're going to provide. This will pay massive dividends down the line. As we will see in ASF 4, this is where the structure of the Professional Services Agreement is so powerful. It forces us to understand and come to mutual agreement on the value to be received PRIOR to beginning the service.

Essentially, you need to uncover your client's emotional drivers during the sales conversation. You want to find out exactly what is driving their decisions on a deeper emotional level than just that they want to save money on their taxes. One of the ways to accomplish this is to ask "why" questions. This is where you continue to parrot back your client's answer in the form of a why question until you get to the true emotional driver behind their decision. Somewhere between five and seven times seems to be the magic number.

Here's an example:

Sales Conversation

Prospective client: "I'd like you to do my taxes for me."

#1 - Accountant: "Why would you like me to do your taxes for you?"

Prospective client: "Because my previous accountant did a crappy job."

#2 – Accountant: "Why do you feel your previous accountant did a crappy job?"

Prospective client: "They just filed my taxes without giving me any business advice."

#3 - Accountant: "Why did you want them to give you business advice?"

Prospective client: "I've been struggling over the last few years to grow my business and I really need help."

#4 - Accountant: "Why are you wanting to grow your business?"

Prospective client: "I'm getting sick and tired of not making more money."

#5 - Accountant: "Why do you want to make more money?"

Prospective client: "I want to make more money so I can provide a better life for my family."

#6 - Accountant: "Why do you want to provide a better life for your family?"

Prospective client: "I want my family to feel safe and protected and taken care of."

#7 - Accountant: "Why do you want your family to feel safe and protected and taken care of?"

Prospective client: "My father was never there for me. He left my family when I was little and I watched my mom struggle to provide for us. I never want to be like him."

Clearly not all conversations will go like this on a first meeting, but you get the picture. Most accountants stay on the surface and never get into the real issues driving their clients and, more importantly, driving where true value comes from. From the example above, now imagine telling the client that your services are specifically designed to ensure the client has full access to your timely advice, whenever they need it, without getting hit with an additional invoice. You are going to be that person who is there for them, and they can count on you to help them grow their business (unlike their father who left them). How much will they be willing to pay for your services now?

People buy with emotion and rationalize that buying decision with logic. This is where the traditional business model is backwards (see Deadly Sin #2). You always want to trigger an emotional response in your client during the sales conversation. This will always drive up value in their eyes. As soon as you're confident you've hit the emotional drivers, you can move on to the price. You're going to WANT to talk about the price as close to the emotional feeling as possible. Good feelings = value = you get paid incredibly well. Again, as we will see in the next section, the Professional Services Agreement ensures that we talk about the price during the sales conversation (and not after, as the traditional model does). Before we get to that, however, let's talk about another integral strategy to use when you're having the sales conversation with your client.

4 Planning Pillars™

The key to delivering maximum value to our clients is to move ourselves up the Value Curve. The best possible position on the curve is that of our client's financial CFO (or financial quarterback). How do we do that? We do that through a 4 *Planning Pillars*™ strategy.

Every one of your clients, whether consciously or not, is building their life based on their own wishes and specifications. It's like building a house. In a simple house design, you have a roof that is supported by four pillars. We can think of your client's life the same way, with those four pillars representing one of their critical planning areas.

Business Plan, Wealth Plan, Retirement Plan & Estate Plan

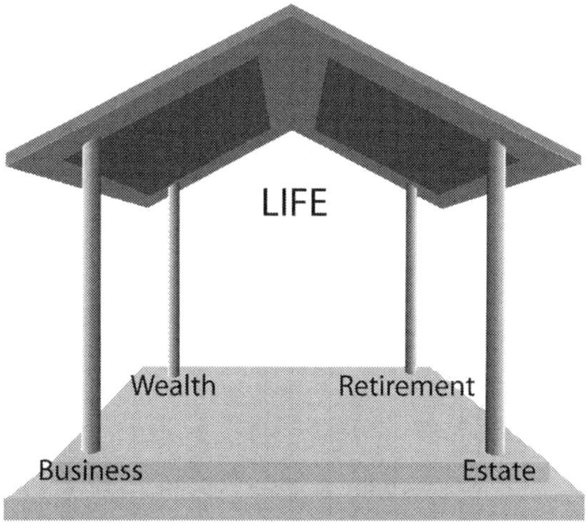

CLIENT'S PLANNING

Anyone who understands basic physics knows that each one of these pillars is connected to the other three in a critical way. If they aren't in alignment with one another, the integrity of the house will be compromised. Ultimately, there has to be an overall plan in place to make sure the house is being built properly. That job normally falls to the general contractor (or in our case the external CFO—the "quarterback"). Without someone at the helm of this project, the house could (and often does) turn out to be a terrible mess.

Picture the plumber, drywallers, electricians, roofers, etc. building each component of the house with their own version of what they think the client needs. This is what normally happens to your client's life when their lawyer, financial advisor, accountant, and business advisor take off in different directions without working together on a cohesive overall plan. Unlike a house that is built once and is rarely renovated, your client's life is constantly changing and evolving, which requires consistently evolving plans to support it. Who's watching over this to ensure the house is being built correctly?

Normally this "general contractor" position falls to the clients themselves. But unlike the general contractor, your client doesn't have the technical expertise to know if all the specifications are being followed and are connecting with one another. Have you ever had a client come to you after the fact and tell you their wills were redone only to find that they're missing critical key tax-planning elements? No, I'm sure that never happens, right? This used to drive me nuts.

The same challenges happen with business, wealth, and retirement plans. Even though we may not be aware of it, these plans may have inconsistencies within them. It's because no one is making sure all of these plans are working together correctly to get our clients to where they want to be with their lives. The tragic part is that most clients don't even realize that they are the ones who have taken this general contractor role on by default.

To be fair, it isn't our client's fault this happens. It's ours. I know it becomes a finger-pointing exercise to say it's the other professionals' fault, but it's really our fault. We need to advise our clients of the problems that can occur with multiple professional plans and no overseer. The client doesn't even realize they need a general contractor (or quarterback) and no one is better qualified to handle the financial quarterback position for our clients than we are, their accountant.

One quick look into the four planning areas and we can easily see where inconsistencies and problems occur. Our professional training, tax knowledge, and financial experience set us up to be our clients' #1 trusted advisor. All we have to do is step up to the plate and make them aware of the benefits of having us oversee these areas, and most importantly, the cost of not having us fulfill this role. Your clients don't know what they don't know. It's your role to educate them on the value of your financial quarterback services and the cost of standing still.

This is an incredibly powerful visualization tool to bring out during your sales conversation. In fact, you'll want to incorporate it into your entire system, as its simplicity and effectiveness in delivering true value to your clients is unmatched. Help them get their life to where they want it to be. This is what clients truly want their accountants to do for them. It's not about tax returns and financial statements. It's about building a life that suits their wishes. Again, they don't really care about what we do; they only care about what they get as a result of what we do.

Now that you've determined your positioning in the market, are managing your client inventory, and have the strategies to sell your services, you need to capture the true value you're going to be bringing to your clients. This leads us into one of my favourite sections of the Accountant Success Formula™: The ASF 4 – Professional Services Agreement.

ASF 4 – Professional Services Agreement (How)

Stop Chasing the Money

We have seen the downside of chasing efficiencies with low-level compliance services and how we have to position ourselves for future success. We've also seen how the billable hour is truly no longer a fit for today's accountant or their clients. The market is showing us where the trend is going, and we can see the tsunami of technology coming down on us. It's now time to secure our new positioning and to negate the effects of the past pains of the billable hour model. It's time to get great, consistent cash flow while capturing the maximum value we're providing our clients. It's time to stop chasing the money. It's time for our new business model. It's time for a new Professional Services Agreement (PSA).

The main driver in a PSA model is a monthly subscription price as opposed to a billable hour method of charging for services. Bundle all your services together, provide your client unlimited access to call you if and when they need, and lock it up with a monthly price. The monthly amount is agreed to during the sales conversation with your prospective client. This naturally forces the conversation to turn to the perceived value of what you're providing, along with a mutual agreement as to the price that is to be paid in light of that perceived value. One of the great things that comes from this method of billing is that it will make you better at selling your services.

It requires you to dig deep into what your clients really want as a result of your services so that you can get your price in alignment with that value they're going to receive.

A monthly subscription model is what consumers love. It removes all surprises and stressors for them. They know exactly what they are going to pay for the service you're performing, it provides them the freedom to call you when they need you, and it gives them a smoothing of their own cash flow. Clients love this model.

More importantly, you'll love the model as well:

- No more time sheets (goodbye WIP reports)
- No more stressing about what to bill after the fact
- No more client pushback on fees after you've done the work
- No more asking the client permission to pay for what you've already done
- No more chasing outstanding A/R
- No more inconsistent cash flow
- No more capital requirements to support WIP & A/R

Another wonderful bi-product is the effect this has on your practice valuation. Cash flow is everything in business, and your predictable, consistent cash-flow model will pay huge dividends when you go to exit your practice.

Everybody wins. I've seen it over and over again. Every time one of my coaching clients adopts this updated model, they greatly increase their cash flow, profitability, and overall sense of peace and enjoyment in their practices. The billable hour model is like a monkey on our back. It's not until it's gone that you feel the relief come off your shoulders. Damn monkeys!

Pricing

There is a wonderful side effect that comes with your client's relief of removing the billable hour model as well. They will happily pay higher fees. The good feelings they get from knowing the pricing ahead of time, having the ability to call you when they need, and having smooth cash outflow is extremely valuable to them. The PSA has value in and of itself. You can charge a premium for this "peace of mind". Remember, the only thing anyone buys is good feelings, and this billing model delivers just that.

The ability to command a premium price using the PSA is not just a theory, it really works. One of my first coaching clients was a CPA named Andrew. He was a partner in a firm in the interior of British Columbia, Canada. He closed his first PSA model client at a 73% higher annual fee than he would have received under the old billable hour model. The best part about this was that he closed this client within 24 hours of our first meeting together. A 73% increase in fees within 24 hours. He was literally jumping through the phone he was so excited. Since then, he hasn't looked back. These results are consistently happening for my clients, again and again and again.

CFO Positioning

Couple this good feeling billing model with the good feelings of your new positioning as their quarterback, their general contractor, and their external CFO, and something magical happens. Price sensitivity drops and your value in the eyes of your clients skyrocket. It's the one, two, three knockout punch of the sales conversation, unlike the Five-Finger Death Punch of the old business model. (Sorry…couldn't help myself. I had to mention my favourite band at least one more time before the end of the book.)

How do you capture this increase in value without reliving the headaches of the old model? You do that by bundling all your services together, agreeing to the price ahead of time, and pulling that amount from your client's bank account through a pre-authorized debit system you control. You get paid what you're worth, you stop chasing the money, and you start receiving the benefits of all your years of hard work.

ASF 5 – Referral Network (Who & What)

This is where you get to pour gasoline on the fire of your practice. Once you have positioned yourself in the market, cleaned your client inventory, learned how to effectively sell your services and captured your worth through a PSA, you are ready to crank up the heat. It's great to have all this in place, however if you're not feeding the machine, it isn't going to do you any good. Welcome to your Referral Network.

I'm sure you've already figured out, I'm not one to go with the tide and follow the herd of lemmings off the cliff. I'm not going to tell you to use all the latest marketing techniques and technology-driven social connection apps to generate leads into your practice. Nope. As my coach and good friend Chris Flett of Ghost CEO™ says, "We're going to use a sniper approach to business development, not a shotgun approach" (www.ghostceo.com).

Clients

Let's hit the nail on the head here. There's a law of attraction that has been proven scientifically. It's not just a new-age, "woo-woo" concept. Ever heard the phrase, "Birds of a feather flock together"? Well, there's a reason why it's a saying. It's true. Like people attract like people. This is another HUGE reason cleaning your inventory of X- and C-level clients is so important. You're not going to attract great clients if you keep a bunch of shitty clients. Those you are trying to attract will smell those bad birds a mile away. So, clean that inventory!

Access your untapped asset in your A- and B-level clients. Asking for a referral is the easiest way to bring this flock together. Your top-level clients hang with top-level people. Successful people surround themselves with successful people. That's just the nature of it. So ask them for a like-minded referral. It's so easy, yet so many accountants have such a difficult time with this. They don't want to look needy and desperate in front of their clients. They want to look successful. The thought of asking their clients for a referral just feels wrong.

It's not asking for the referral that's the problem. It's HOW you're asking for the referral that makes you look needy and desperate. If you're not originating new business, you're not building a successful practice. If you're not hungry for new business, someone else is going to get it from you. If you're not asking your existing clients for a referral, you're ignoring the low-hanging fruit right in front of your nose. Didn't I mention that accountants generally suck at sales? The same goes for asking for a referral from their existing client base.

There is a fine line here. If you're constantly asking for referrals, you will look needy and desperate. Nobody wants to do business with a business owner that is needy. Needy is creepy. Even more importantly, there's another negative impact on your clients if you don't ask for a referral in the right way. Your clients also have an underlying concern that if you are constantly taking on new clients, you'll be too busy to handle their needs. "Leave room for me" is all they'll be thinking.

Here's how to ask your clients for a referral that will ensure they don't see you as needy and that their service levels won't suffer. It's quite simple really. Tell them you've recently let some clients go as they were no longer a fit in your practice, that you have a few spots available and are looking to fill them with great clients just like them. If they have any friends or business colleagues who would fit your unique service offering and value model, you would be happy to welcome them into your practice.

There are a few key items I'd like to note here about this approach:

#1 – It positions you as an exclusive firm. You don't just take on anyone. This hits on a key mental trigger in sales…scarcity. In simple economics, you know that the scarcer something is, the higher the price can be commanded.

#2 – It shows you are not starving for work. Needy is creepy, and above all, no one wants to work with an accounting firm that is desperate for clients. People want a successful accountant looking after their financial affairs. Imagine the thought of having an accountant doing work for you while you know that their own business is suffering. No thanks; I'll go somewhere else please.

#3 – It shows you are consciously aware of their needs. Your existing client will be more motivated to send you a referral because you have managed your inventory of clients to ensure their service levels don't decline. Nothing worse than having your accountant have too much work on their plate so they can't focus on your stuff, right? Sound familiar?

Overall, great existing clients are an amazing referral source for any accounting practice. All you need to do is ask them. But be careful HOW you ask them. How you ask them makes all the difference between helping and hurting your accounting practice.

Other Professional Advisors (PA's)

The second source of great client referrals is your network of other Professional Advisors (or PA's, as I like to call them). Lawyers, financial advisors, insurance brokers, business coaches, and the like are a gold mine when managed properly. The greatest clients come from great referrals, and this pool of professionals is the one of the best. You want to swim with these people. They multiply your reach 100-fold given their daily interaction with your ideal clients.

Just like with existing clients, professional advisors must be approached with care and caution. You can't just go hog wild asking every single PA to send you clients. You know how much you'd like that yourself, right? Simply go to a local Chamber of Commerce event and you'll experience what I'm talking about. People running around like chickens with their heads cut off, throwing their business cards at every single person they meet. Two minutes into meeting you for the first time and they're diving right in, asking you if you have any clients for them.

No, the PA's I'm talking about are those your clients are currently using. This is the motherload. I'm continually amazed at how many accountants leave this resource untapped. When working with my coaching clients, we go through their client inventory and refer it back to what I call The Doctor's File™. This is a proprietary source document that houses all of the client's critical information. And none is more critical than the details of who your existing clients other PA's are. Whenever an accountant complains to me about not being able to find great clients, I always ask, "When was the last time you connected with your existing clients' PA's?" Deer in the headlights and the sound of crickets is all I get.

How do we approach this valuable Referral Network resource? Well, let's look back to our positioning again. We are now going to be acting in that all-so-critical role of our client's financial quarterback, the external CFO or general contractor. We are going to understand and ensure our client's four plans (pillars of their home) are in alignment with one another so as to ensure their life is built to their specifications.

So where are we going to get the information required to properly understand these four plans? The client's other professional advisors, of course. You will naturally have to connect and communicate with these people to get their insight into the plans in place. Just talking to your client about these four plans is not enough. You'll never get a clear picture on what's really happening, nor will you be serving yourself by not discussing these pillars directly with the other PA's.

You must be careful how you engage this group. If you thought clients were sensitive, you haven't seen anything until you've rubbed another PA the wrong way. There are greater egos at play here and greater stakes. One wrong interaction with a key PA can spread like wildfire and permanently damage your referral source. And this works both ways. I remember one time doing what I considered to be a simple estate freeze for a construction client of mine. The lawyer they had didn't play nice in the sandbox, to say the least. It was painful working with them, and many times I seriously questioned whether the file would ever get completed. Needless to say, I never referred anyone to that firm again.

Often, negative interactions can be subtle, and you might miss them. You never want to bruise a PA's ego. It's the type of gift that keeps on giving… in the worst way possible. As we're positioning ourselves with our client and approaching these other PA's, we need to be cautious to ensure we are forging strong alliances. Think of every interaction with your client's PA's as an investment into the success of your accounting practice. Follow these quick guidelines as you engage this group.

You're Not the Quarterback

Never ever, never, ever tell the PA's that you are their client's financial quarterback! I know I told you to position yourself in your client's eyes that way, but don't throw that into the face of the other PA's. This will rub them the wrong way. How would you feel hearing from your client's lawyer that they are now the client's CFO and they're going to check over your work to make sure it's being done correctly? No, no, no. This would be bad, very bad.

You always want the PA to feel you're on the same professional level with your mutual clients. Nothing is worse than a pissing match between advisors. You always work *with* them for your clients benefit. Never EVER tell them you're taking the control away from them. All you are doing is getting a clear picture of your mutual client's four plans to ensure that what you're doing is in alignment. That's what you tell them. You're always looking for collaboration; never take an "I'm in charge over you" type of stance.

Enhance Them

Another key aspect to working with other professional advisors has to do with your motive around their service offering and positioning. As much as we are looking to enhance you and your firm, you want to be looking to do the same for the other PA's. This not only enhances the value to your client, but it pays huge dividends when it comes to having referrals flow your way.

Think about it for a minute. How quickly are you going to send a PA one of your great clients without knowing how the PA performs in action? Not likely—they may be a complete disaster. You'll never know until you work with them. What's equally important is how they experience the working relationship. Here's the key: When working with a mutual client, always be looking to enhance their service offering and positioning as well. Most accountants make the critical mistake of trying to reduce other PA's' work, thinking it will impress the client by reducing their costs. Accountants are so fixated on cost reduction. Sometimes I wonder if it was something that happened to us in childhood. Many hours of therapy needed here, for sure.

This approach is so powerful it will make you stand out in a sea of accountants. Through the grapevine, we heard about a certain lawyer in town who was telling their clients they never refer anyone to accountants. I they had been traumatized by repeated failures. Clearly, therapy is required for lawyers too…(no, I'm not touching that topic with a ten-foot pole). Anyways, she did start referring to our firm. This was after she had experienced working with us on a mutual client's estate plan. We took the approach of learning clearly the *4 Planning Pillars*™ of our client, and we worked with all the other PA's involved to make our mutual client's Life Plan come together. Throughout the engagement, we found ways to expand the lawyer's involvement in the big picture, as well as ways she could do even more valuable work with her client. She was so shocked and impressed by our approach that we became her only accounting referral source. Now that's positioning in the market, being her ONLY referral source!

You may have noticed I haven't even mentioned the most obvious approach to getting referrals from other PA's. Simply sending them referrals would seem the easiest way to get referrals back, right? I haven't commented on it because it's too obvious and less effective. Firing referrals back and forth doesn't mean great referrals, and you want great referrals, not just warm bodies. The real key to impressing other PA's, and getting great referrals from them, is to show them how amazing it is to work alongside you with their great mutual clients. Nothing will impress a PA more than finding ways to enhance their service offering and making them look great in front of their clients.

The ASF 5

To recap, these are the five components of the Accountant Success Formula™.

Positioning
Inventory
Sales
Professional Service Agreements
Referral Network

I have my coaching clients put this list somewhere they can clearly see it so that they are continually referring back to these steps. Determine your **Positioning**, clean and maintain your client **Inventory**, remember **Sales** (what you actually sell and how you sell it), capture your true value and stop chasing the money through a **Professional Services Agreement** and finally, keep a steady stream of great client referrals coming your way through your **Referral Network**.

Before I conclude our time together and send you off into the great big blue horizon of your new business model, I'd like to cover a very important topic. It's well and good to know what you need to do here with the ASF 5, but there's a critical piece of the puzzle missing. The most important asset of your practice is your client inventory. Without clients, you don't even have a practice—as such, the next chapter is completely dedicated to expanding on this topic. It's not just important bringing clients on to your new model, it's equally important that you move bad inventory clients off as well.

CHAPTER 6: Onboarding (and Offloading) Clients

Introduction

One of the greatest feelings I ever had in my accounting practice was onboarding a new client. What was really surprising to me, then, was the amazing feeling I used to get from offloading clients that no longer fit in my practice. It's one of the most cleansing and therapeutic things you can do for your practice. But whether it's onboarding or offloading clients, you need certain skills to make it happen in a way that's going to truly benefit your practice. Done the wrong way, it can take away from your practice's value instead of enhancing it. Clients really are the lifeblood of any accounting practice, so utmost care should always be in the forefront of your mind.

There are really only two types of clients for your practice: new and existing. I'm going to cover how to onboard each of these separately. We'll follow that with the timing you're going to want to take with respect to each type of client and the overall process you're about to undertake. Lastly, I'll go over off-boarding clients. This is traditionally one of the hardest things any accountant has to do. The thought of "losing" clients is a major fear for most accountants. So the idea of purposefully sending them on their way can be too much to comprehend. However, if you're going to build a great practice, you can't be fooling yourself about the value of your inventory. You can't be keeping bad apples in the bunch. To start, however, let's get to onboarding new and existing clients into your new model.

Onboarding New Clients

Set Your Pricing

There are numerous combinations to get your practice to your revenue targets (see 5 Ways to $600K). Before you start onboarding new clients, determine a new normal for yourself. Remember the value you'll be creating for these new clients, and write out the numbers of clients you'll be taking on and at what price point. All new clients will have to be at this "new normal" or minimum entry to be admitted to your practice from this point forward.

Remember back to our Pareto Principle (the 80/20 rule). 80% of our results will come from 20% of our clients. We want to focus our energies on this 20%. These are your ideal clients. These are the clients that bring you results in your practice. These are the clients you want. If we're only looking for those 20%, we want to be pricing as high as possible to weed out the bottom 80%. This leads us to a response you're going to want to hear when you're onboarding new clients. That response is the word "No".

Yes, you heard me correctly. You want to hear the word "No". You don't want to hear it too much, but you do want to hear it. If you heard no all the time, you'd have no practice at all. But on the flip side, if you never hear the word no and you close 100% of your clients, then you're leaving money on the table. I used to cringe when I would walk through my sales conversation, hit the key pain points for the prospective client, and get mutual buy-in on the value, only to then quote them a price that they would instantly say "Yes" to. Damn, I left money on the table!

Track your closing rates with new clients. You can't manage what you can't measure. Memory is hazy at best, but numbers don't lie. The proof will be in the numbers, so track this and monitor your progress. If you're not getting any "No's", then increase your new entry-level prices and start again. The higher the price per client, the fewer clients you need in your practice to make your revenue target. The fewer clients, the less work and stress you will have, and the more successful you'll be.

Never Drop Your Price

When meeting with new clients, be prepared to meet people who will say they want to work with you but will ask for a lower monthly price. The amazing value you're now bringing them will be unlike any other accountant they've encountered, and they'll want the benefits, but they'll balk at the price. Resist the urge to reduce the monthly minimum to accommodate these people. Never, ever drop your price. It's the kiss of death.

If they can't pay, or won't pay, that's fine. Let them go. Like fishing, you have to throw back the small fish. You have limited seats on your plane, and you are looking to increase the size of your first-class and business-class sections. Discounting has so many negative impacts, and you're no longer playing in that out-dated business model. You're looking for clients who see your value and have the means to pay for that value. Let some other accountant work with the rest.

Stay the Course

Accountants are creatures of habit, and no habit is more ingrained than that of the old business model. Keep your guard up, and watch yourself for slipping back into old patterns. Discounting your fees is just one of them. There are many bad habits lurking in the shadows. Stay the course and remember your Why. You're in this to build something great, not to stay stuck in the old model and continue to suffer. You've done that long enough. Change your habits; change your life.

Breaking bad habits and replacing them with new ones will take time. It's like working out a muscle. You need to retrain it to do something different; this takes discipline, persistence, and patience. The purpose of this new habit is to give you more time, money, and freedom in your practice, and you will get there but only if you stay the course. Onboard your new clients with your new minimum price, make sure they're adding value to your practice, and accept "no's" as a sign that you're capturing the maximum value you can for the services you're providing.

Onboarding Existing Clients

This one takes more effort and causes accountants the most stress. It is also why it is the most important to deal with. The harder the task is, the more valuable. Nothing comes for free, and onboarding existing clients is no exception. As with any unknown, the fear disappears once you've encountered it a number of times and turned it into the known. What you will quickly find once you start engaging your existing clients is that they love this new model. It literally sells itself.

Set Your Pricing

You'll need to set a new minimum price before you begin. In most cases, this new pricing level will be lower than your new client pricing level. This is natural, as fear grips most accountants thinking about how they are going to make their existing clients jump to their new client minimum pricing. This is okay. You nevertheless still need a minimum pricing level to strive to bring them up to.

Without a tangible target level for pricing, you'll be a flimsy reed that is being pulled in the direction of the water current. When pressures hit, you'll keep adjusting your pricing all over the map, and that doesn't serve you. Pick a new minimum level, and make that your goal. Simply model out the results of this new minimum level to see what your revenue levels will look like once you onboard your existing clients at this new minimum. Nothing like looking at the hard numbers to get you motivated!

Face Your Fears

Ultimately, you need to face your fears about introducing this new business model (and new pricing levels) to your existing clients. Here's where the rubber meets the road. What if they say no? Let's be honest with ourselves, they fully have the right to say no. And if they do, what happens? Will your practice go bankrupt? Will you no longer be able to pay your staff or overhead? Or even worse, pay yourself? Come on, get serious—the mind game is the hardest part.

Our experience shows that a super majority, upwards of 98% of clients, say, "Hell yes!" They love this new model. Removing the unknown annual invoice, smoothing out their cash flow, and giving them unlimited access to you is like a breath of fresh air. It's like sending love after years of abuse. They will welcome it with open arms.

Re-Positioning Opportunity

With this new billing model comes your opportunity to expand the value you can bring your clients. Over and over again, we see clients leaving their accountants due to poor advice. More importantly, they leave because of the lack of advice they didn't even ask for. Yes, that's exactly it. Advice they didn't ask for. Clients want to be led. It's up to you to provide your clients with the advice they desperately need, but don't even know they need. Go back to your *4 Planning Pillars* ™ and show them what they need and what you're now going to provide.

This increased positioning will naturally accommodate an increase in price. As you move yourself up the Value Curve, price sensitivity reduces, and perceived value increases. The conversation you'll have with your existing clients will give you the opportunity to not only reposition yourself, it will give you the opportunity to capture more value and ultimately a higher price.

One of my coaching clients, DP, was having his first few transition conversations with his existing clients. Naturally, he was mindful of what his clients would say and more importantly how much more he could charge them. After only three meetings, he was completely convinced. His clients loved the model. Not only that, he started to secure up to 64% increases in annual fees as a result of his new positioning. His clients loved the new expanded model and the *4 Pillars Planning*™ approach.

Stay the Course

Just like with onboarding new clients, be sure to stay the course. Expect some no's along the way, and take them in stride. I'll cover how to deal with offloading clients in more detail later on, but for now, accept that a few will say no, and you'll have to let them go. Remember what you're building here. Resists the urge to keep some clients on the old model. Those that get it will get it, and those that don't, won't. So move on. Don't sacrifice the good of the many for the whims of the few. You're building a practice that will serve your clients, your staff, and yourself the way you all deserve. Resist the dark side of the force! (I knew I could get another Star Wars reference in somewhere.)

I know how hard it is to resist keeping some clients on the old model. As I was implementing and testing this in my own practice, I fell into the trap of letting some clients stay on the old model, for fear of losing them. This short-term avoidance is a long-term pain in the ass. What quickly becomes apparent is that the anguish of keeping some on the old model and some on the new model becomes too much to bear. Every time you have to record, analyze, and bill out WIP for these few clients, you will become increasingly agitated. You'll become hypersensitive to how bad the old model is, and you won't want to tolerate it. Save yourself the headache and stay the course.

Timing

The next thing to talk about is timing. Onboarding clients onto this new model is great, but you need to be aware of when to make it most effective. As we all know, it's one thing to understand what to do and another to actually implement it.

First Things First

When do you start onboarding? Clearly you should do your foundation work first. You want to have a clear picture of who your new ideal client will be, what price point you're going to make as your new minimum (new and existing clients) and have all your backend agreements and pre-authorized debit systems in place. Even more importantly, however, is that you need to practice your sales conversation.

Practicing this communication before testing it out on your client is critical. Start by practicing on your own, and go through your new model highlights. Next, role-play it with your business partner, staff, or spouse. You may feel silly about this, but nothing prepares you for game-time more than practice. I run through practice sessions with my coaching clients, and it really helps get the kinks out before they start going live.

New Clients

You've done your foundation work, you've practiced the new sales conversation, and you're ready to go. Get at it. When it comes to onboarding new clients, you can, and should, do it right away. It's also another great practice ground for honing your sales conversation and positioning. There's less mental resistance to trying out something new with someone you just met vs. trying it with an existing client. Time and time again, I hear from my coaching clients that their apprehension quickly dissolved after the first few conversations in new client meetings.

Hearing a no from a new client is not nearly as painful as hearing it from an existing one. This is where you can practice hearing that "dreaded" word (yes, I'm being sarcastic again!). You want to hear that word. Remember, if you're not getting any "no's" with your new pricing, then you're leaving money on the table. Onboarding new clients is a great way to test the market to see if you're doing that or not. As we shall see in the off-loading section, once you start landing a few higher-end-priced clients, you'll get a double win: you'll be able to get rid of multiple lower-end clients at the same time. Increased revenues coupled with a reduced workload is a beautiful combination.

Existing Clients

Once you've had your first taste of success with onboarding new clients, when do you start with your existing clients? The best time, for multiple reasons, is during your year-end review. Go through your standard Five-Finger Death Punch routine, and then immediately go into the new model. Nothing highlights the benefits of this updated business model than presenting it right after putting your client through the pain of the old model.

Sign them up on the spot. Have their Professional Services Agreement completed and ready to sign during the year-end review. Assume "yes". As the saying goes: Strike while the iron is hot. This also has the added benefit of front-end-loading your cash flow in the first year of implementation with your existing clients. You'll have a doubling up happen in the first year. Full year-end bill plus the PSA monthly cash flow. This is where you can easily expect to have an increase of over 50% in your billings in year one.

The other benefit of onboarding your clients individually is that you can spread it out over the course of a year. You also really want to have these conversations face to face if possible. Firing out a boatload of PSA's to every single client without having a direct sales conversation is going to dramatically reduce your closing rates. I know I said you want to hear "no's", but you don't want to artificially increase that no rate just because you didn't want to have a direct conversation with your client about the new model.

Once you get a majority of your clients onboard and you've got extra time on your hands, you may start to accelerate the process and meet with your clients prior to the year-end meeting. Ultimately, the quicker you get clients onto this model, the better in the longer run. In business, you're always looking to maximize the lifetime value of your client. In some cases, I will recommend to my coaching clients to forgo their year-end bill to lock their client up with an even higher monthly PSA. What seems like a scary proposition at first quickly becomes clear when I show them the numbers. Timed right, you can be easily up in total revenue within 12 months or less.

I had a great corporate client who was paying me around $6,000/year under the old model. I remember calling him a few months before the year-end review started and having the new model conversation with him. I told him he wouldn't get a year-end bill for this year and locked him into a monthly PSA for $750/month ($9,000/year). For this particular client,

I didn't increase any services, I just sold him on the PSA. Had I waited to present the PSA at the year-end meeting, I was probably going to go in around $575/month ($6,600/year). But, because I was selling him on not having to pay a year-end bill, I was willing to do $750/month. Do the cash flow over a couple of years, and I would be break even, but past that I was making an extra $2,400/year on this client. Remember to play the long game. Go for maximizing the lifetime value of the client, and don't be tempted to take the quick, easy money.

Probably one of the hardest things an accountant can do is cull their client inventory. But nothing is more important to the health and financial wellbeing of one's accounting practice. Ignore this step, and you'll be dooming yourself to the same old grind, year after year. What's amazing though is that once you get a taste of saying, "No, it's time for you to go" to clients, you'll be hooked. I think I loved this almost as much as landing a new client.

Offloading Clients

The immediate effects are great. It will feel like a weight has been lifted off your shoulders. It's like a hidden burden you didn't realize was there has finally been removed, and you feel the lightness of free movement. The long-term results are incredible. Removing clients that no longer fit your model frees up so much of your time and mental energy. Once they're gone, you'll be more creative, happy, and free. Yes, it almost sounds like a spiritual experience. For some, it kind of is.

Just think about how much you think about clients. I can't count how many times I would be just about falling asleep when those invasive thoughts would creep into my mind and jolt me awake.

- Did the XYZ Company tax return get filed on time?
- Where is that missing information from Jerk Incorporated?
- When is Cheap Bastard Inc. going to pay my outstanding invoice?

All these clients take time and energy away from you. It's time to let them go so you can have a good night's sleep. Ultimately, every client you have rents a space in your brain. And this is high-priced real estate! Someone should have to pay you for you to even THINK about them. Once you clean these out, you'll sleep like a baby.

Two Important Points

You've done your inventory of clients and have categorized them into A, B, C, and X clients. We're now going to deal with these C's & X's properly. But before we do, I want to cover two important points. There are two overriding things you want to keep in mind as you're offloading these clients, and both of them will impact your bottom line either positively or negatively. Control what you can control, and the exit is something you definitely want and need to control.

The first thing is something my father told me many years ago, when I was working with him in his construction business. He was old school when it came to business (and life). He came to Canada from Norway in the summer of '69 with only $20 to his name (any Brian Adams fans out there get the reference?). He knew how to work hard, and learned how to build a successful business. He was dealing with a real jerk of a sub trade on the site. After the guy left, I asked him why he didn't just kick the guy off the job when he first started acting up. My dad said, "I didn't have to. Remember, there's always a way to tell someone to go to hell, where they look forward to the trip."

Rule #1 – when offloading clients, send them on their way where they are actually looking forward to the trip.

Rule #2 – Just because these clients are no longer a fit for you doesn't mean they're not a fit for another accountant.

With coaching clients of the Accountant Success Formula™, we ensure we have set up a referral arrangement with another firm where we can send these clients for a trailing revenue share. Of course, depending on your professional governing rules, referral fees may need to be structured in a certain way, but there are almost inevitably ways to get paid for sending clients someone's way. Getting paid for clients you offload is like icing on the cake.

X Clients

Let's start with your clients in the X column. These are those messy, shitty files, or clients with bad personalities that just don't mesh with you. Every firm has them. And what continually amazes me is that every firm keeps them! What's wrong with accountants anyways? Keeping these types of clients is like being involved in the oldest profession in humankind. Yes, I just said that again. It's like getting paid to get "_____".

What's worse is that many of these X-type clients are the worst payers to begin with. So moving to the PSA model should be a quick fix, and we'll now get paid, right? Wrong! Don't keep these clients. You'll be tempted to let them stay for the reason I just mentioned, but it won't do your practice any good in the long run. Shitty clients are shitty clients, and they have to go. Remember your WHY. Stay the course and clean your inventory properly.

When approaching these clients, don't ever give them the option of coming onto the new model. The conversation should simply go like this, "I'm positioning my practice in a new direction and I unfortunately can no longer provide you the level of service you deserve. To make sure you're not left having to look for a new accountant, I have made arrangements with _________ (name of referral firm), and they would be happy to take care of all your accounting needs. I thank you for having had the opportunity to serve you and wish you all the best in the future."

Look forward to the trip, and hello referral fee!

C Clients

Let's now look at your C-level clients. These are low-level clients that aren't necessarily shitty to deal with, nor are the files particularly messy, nor do they pay late. What's very apparent though, is that if you did work for only this level of clients, your business model would look horrendous. Model it out. Hello, 4,000 personal tax returns! You may feel bad about letting them go, but you'll feel even worse if you keep them.

Normally these are the type of clients who, if they could pay your minimum, you'd love to keep them on. So what are you to do with these ones? Again, always remember the two golden rules: send them away looking forward to the trip and give them a new place to land while you get paid. Give them the opportunity to stay, but say it in a way that gives them the option to go. Let them save face. The conversation should go something like this: "I'm positioning my practice in a new direction to be able to better serve my clients. I'm moving away from a billable hour model to a subscription-based model and will be working more closely with my clients through a 4 *Pillars Planning*™ approach. As a result, I have a new minimum pricing level of $x/month…" Wait for a reaction. If it's positive, sign them up. If they react with shock and horror, just act as if you knew their response was going to be that way. Follow up by saying: "I suspected this pricing level wasn't going to be a fit for you. I didn't want you to feel left abandoned in finding a new accountant, so I've made arrangements with (name of referral firm), and they would be happy to take care of you. I thank you for having had the opportunity to serve you and wish you all the best in the future."

Look forward to the trip, and hello referral fee!

Closing Thoughts

Onboarding clients into the new model and off-loading clients onto greener pastures feels great. Whether they're coming or going, they win and you win. You'll start to feel empowered and realize that you are the one in charge of your practice. Those clients who stay will love what you provide for them and will be happy to pay your fees. Those that don't will be happy knowing you've taken care of their best interests in finding them a replacement accountant to take care of them. Good feelings all around.

What's your new accounting practice going to look like in the future? That is exactly the picture I'm going to paint for you in the final chapter. This is your new future, one that you get to control and design according to your wishes and not the hangover of the old-school model. This is the new vision for you.

CHAPTER 7: A Vision for You

Think back to why you became a professional accountant in the first place. What was it about the profession that you were drawn to? Was it the respect you would get, or the great money you thought you would make, or was it being able to help people with their financial needs? For me, thinking back on what that longhaired kid in the late eighties was feeling, the answer would have been all of the above. It was also a feeling of relief that I knew what I wanted to do when I grew up. One look at my office, and you'd have to question whether I have grown up yet! Star Wars Legos® and electric guitars still adorn my walls (again, the subject of perhaps another book).

What were your reasons for this choice? There was something that made you decide to become an accountant, and more importantly, to run your own practice. The thoughts of working with appreciative clients, making great money, and having time and freedom to enjoy your life were most likely what you had envisioned. So what happened? Why hasn't this dream materialized for so many professional accountants? For many, the lure of the profession has felt like being a moth to a flame. They feel burned and, most importantly, burnt out and bitter with where they're at and what they have to endure year after year. What the hell happened?

You've Been Lied To

Yes, you've been lied to. The accounting profession has lied to you. All those accountants who came before us lied to us and conditioned us to believe that our accounting lives had to be burdened with long, gruelling hours and that the stress of the billable hour model was the "professional and ethical" way to charge our clients. They lied because they were lied to themselves. For a group of supposedly intelligent individuals, the profession has done a piss-poor job of improving the lives of future accountants. Where other industries have evolved and adapted to the changing needs of their customers, the professional accounting sector has stayed stagnant and unmoving in its resolve to hold on to an outdated business model that is no longer a fit.

A few, however, have seen the writing on the wall and have broken free from this enslavement to the status quo. For some, it takes the pain of living with the old model to finally say enough is enough. For others, it takes a life-changing event to shake them up to start looking for a better way. For me, it took the extreme pain of the breakup of my first partnership to snap me awake to the insanity of how I'd been working. I didn't see it at the time, but today I am so grateful for having received that slap in the face that woke me up.

The change it made to my life when I updated the business model in my practice was invaluable. I felt like that longhaired kid again, filled with the excitement of future possibilities, and I finally started to reap the rewards of all my years of hard work. I made more money than I ever thought possible in an accounting practice, and I had the time and freedom to actually enjoy it! The stress relief of no longer following the billable hour model was the icing on the cake. I never realized how bad the stress was until it was removed. I have a new appreciation for the phrase "having a monkey on your back". You really don't realize it's there until it's gone.

Today, I now have the privilege of sharing this new updated business model with accountants from all over the globe. So many have been able to get that monkey off their back and start living a life of freedom they envisioned when they first went into the profession. Take my first coaching client, DP. When we first started working together, he had enormous levels of stress. He had a young family and had been hungrily growing his practice for over 10 years. DP was working insane hours, and the stress was taking its toll in every area of his life. He had an unmatched work ethic. Within the first six months of implementing the Accountant Success Formula™, he was looking and acting like a new person. His income shot up dramatically, and most importantly, he took back control of his practice so that it started paying him back in time. He was able to leave the office early and drive his daughter to dance lessons. He was even able to go on a boys' trip to Vegas, in the middle of tax season. Talk about breaking the mould. No one in Vegas believed he was an accountant, and fellow accountants couldn't believe he went!

Life's Too Short...to Work Like an Accountant

Let's get real for a moment. We only have so much time on this earth. This is a limited engagement we have going on here. So why do accountants work the way they do? Sometimes I think we should call it a proud, noble, and insane profession. I serious question the collective sanity of accountants. When you look at the amount of schooling, studying, and training we go through, you'd assume we were intelligent people. And we are, but just not when it comes to seeing how crazy our own profession is.

Many studies have been done on the dying. One of the biggest regrets people have is that they wished they hadn't worked so much. They wish they had spent more time with their loved ones, travelled more, and taken more risks in their life. Those on their deathbeds realize that they wasted their precious years on things that didn't really matter. Life's short, and if we're smart, we'll spend our time on activities that we'll be able to look back on and be thankful for time well spent.

For accountants, we've been brainwashed into thinking that the way we work is just the price we have to pay. We've been conditioned to believe that this is just the way it is. But it's a lie. And sadly, this lie has been stealing away our precious, limited years of life. Life's too short to act like this. Life's too short to have this level of stress. Life's too short to miss out on spending time with loved ones. Life's too short...to work like an accountant.

Break Free

There's an old saying that goes:

> When was the best time to plant a tree?
> **Answer:** 50 years ago.
> When's the next best time?
> **Answer:** Today.

Regardless of how long you've been slogging it out in your practice, you can change. Those accountants closer to retirement age can still update their business model today and reap the rewards of a higher-exit valuation. Those just starting out can build it right from the start. Those at the mid-way point of their careers can pivot and embrace an updated business model and take back control of their lives. It doesn't matter where you are in your journey, you can make changes now for a better future.

Break yourself free from the jail of the old model and step into the freedom of the new. Ultimately, you'll find that you'll be stepping into your own creative power. One of the greatest benefits of the Accountant Success Formula™ is a renewed sense of creativity. The time and freedom you'll gain from this updated business model will give you the space you need to become more creative. You'll find your ability to simply think and discover new solutions for your clients will explode. Being released from the stresses and burdens of the old business model opens up new creative energies you didn't know you had. Creativity needs space to happen. When you free your mind from extraneous stresses you'll have this space. I've seen it happen time and again, accountants regaining their creative powers to unlock incredible value for their practices and their clients.

Reap the Rewards

When you have time to think without being so busy all the time, you'll be able to slow down and smell the flowers. This ability to slow down gives you the perspective to see what you really want from your practice and your life. With this clarity comes the ability to shape where you want your future to go.

You get to choose the direction of your practice. You get to choose how you're going to spend your free time. You get to choose how to live your life.

And really, isn't this why you became a professional accountant in the first place, to be able to live a great life? This is the real reason you're an accountant. You deserve it. Now it's time to claim that life for yourself and reap the rewards of all the hard work and sacrifices you made to become a professional accountant. You can now take control and build your life the way you want it.

Imagine Your Future

Let me paint a picture for you. One that's happening every day to accountants all over the globe:

- Imagine no longer being shackled to long, gruelling hours to make a living.
- Imagine no longer having the stress of tracking your time, issuing invoices, and chasing outstanding accounts receivable.
- Imagine never having to worry if your clients are going to pay your fees.
- Imagine working with great clients who really appreciate the value you provide and, above all, are happy to pay you incredibly well.

- Imagine having smooth, consistent, and predictable cash flow in your practice.
- Imagine being able to buy that dream vacation home and to take holidays when you want to.
- Imagine finally reaping the benefits of all your years of study, sacrifice, and hard work.

I am incredibly grateful for being able to have the opportunity to free so many accountants from the shackles of the outdated model. Seeing the faces of my fellow colleagues light up when they apply the Accountant Success Formula™ to their practices has been the highlight of my professional career. I loved working with business clients in my accounting practice, but nothing compares to the feeling I get seeing the movement that we've started within the profession itself.

Showing accountants the way to a brighter future has an incredible ripple effect as well. It may sound corny, but accountants do change lives. The positive impact it has on their friends and family as well as bringing so much more incredible value to their clients is just the tip of the iceberg. Each life that we touch touches the lives of those they touch. It sets off a chain reaction that literally can impact millions. This is the vision of a great future I have for our accounting profession. One that frees itself first, so that it can give itself to the world it serves.

This future is yours to have. All you need to do is realize that the traditional business model is no longer serving you, and make a decision to take your life back. The Accountant Success Formula™ is for those accountants who realize they need to update their business model to drive profits, attract great clients, and get the time and freedom they deserve. The Accountant Success Formula™ is for you.

Next Steps

There is a saying: *To be successful you need to know where to find the information and how to use it.* I would take that one step further and add that information is completely useless unless you take action.

To get results, you need to take action.

What are the next action steps you're going to take?

You're not alone on this journey to build a great life for yourself. There is a movement of accountants, just like you, who have found the solution, learned how to use it, and taken action to make it a reality.

I now invite you to join us in building that reality for yourself.

Send me an email at Erik@ErikSolbakkenCPA.com, or go to www.ErikSolbakkenCPA.com to find out more about The Accountant Success Formula™ Program and see how we can work together to take action to get you the life you deserve.

Acknowledgements

First of all, I owe a great deal of thanks to the pioneers who came before me: Paul Dunn, Ron Baker, Ric Payne and Mark Lloydbottom. Without you sharing your visions freely, I may never have seen the light and would still be stuck under the old archaic model. Words can't express how much you changed my life. I am forever grateful.

I also want to thank my friend and coach, Chris Flett of Ghost CEO™, for providing me with guidance, insight, and structure. Your "not-so-gentle" nudges kept me on task and on track to completion. Thank you, my friend.

Finally, I'd like to acknowledge my first coaching client, Damon Pallan, CPA. I knew what the Accountant Success Formula™ did for me, but it wasn't until we implemented it into your practice that I realized its true power. Seeing it change your life made me realize I could share it with the world. Thank you for the enthusiasm and willingness to embrace this updated business model.

About the Author

Erik Solbakken is a CPA, Speaker, and Business Advisor, and the Creator of the Accountant Success Formula™. He worked in public practice for over 26 years, providing accounting, tax, and advisory services to incorporated business owners and their families.

He discovered strategies that were so effective that they allowed him to triple his revenues and create a successful accounting practice, which he later sold for a multiple on billings. He now shares these strategies with other accountants around the world in his proven system, showing them how to maximize profits, attract the best clients, and get the time and freedom they deserve.

A thought leader in his field, Erik's system of approaching your accounting practice will show you how to:

Maximize Profit: Stop chasing the money and maximize your profits in a fully leveraged way. Charge what you're worth and make abundant income.

Attract Ideal Clients: Attract the best clients who value you and will gladly pay premium prices for your services. You'll get to selectively choose the clients you engage with and spend time on only the business activities you enjoy.

Create a Life of Freedom: Grow a profitable practice while creating a work/life balance that supports your health and happiness. Work fewer hours and enjoy life more. You'll have time for hobbies, travel, and being with your loved ones.